Open
Between
Us

Poets on Poetry

Donald Hall, General Editor

Open
Between
Us

DAVID IGNATOW

Edited by Ralph J. Mills, Jr.

Ann Arbor   **The University of Michigan Press**

Copyright © by The University of Michigan 1980
All rights reserved
Published in the United States of America by
The University of Michigan Press and simultaneously
in Rexdale, Canada, by John Wiley & Sons Canada, Limited
Manufactured in the United States of America

Library of Congress Cataloging in Publication Data

Ignatow, David, 1914-
   Open between us.

   I. Mills, Ralph J.   II. Title.
PS3517.G5306   818'.5'408   79-23230
ISBN 0-472-06314-6

Acknowledgments

Grateful acknowledgment is made to the following publishers, journals, and libraries for permission to reprint copyrighted material:

Atlantic Review for permission to reprint excerpts from "A Dialogue at Compas" published under the title "On the Poetry of Irrelevance: A Dialogue," *Atlantic Review* (New Series), 1979.

Beloit Poetry Journal for permission to reprint the Introduction to *William Carlos Williams: A Memorial Chapbook.*

Bobbs-Merrill for permission to reprint "The Beginning," from *American Poets in 1976,* edited by William Heyen.

Carleton Miscellany for permission to reprint "L. C. Woodman: A Personal Memory" and "Unfinished Business."

Chelsea 14 (1964) for permission to reprint "Williams's Influence: Some Social Aspects," abridged from an essay written for *Questo e Altro,* Milan.

Hampden-Sydney Poetry Review for permission to reprint "The Biggest Bomb: An Impressionistic Essay."

The Nation for permission to reprint "The Past Reordered" by David Ignatow, April 24, 1967. Copyright 1967 The Nation Associates.

For Lawrence Chauncey Woodman, 1890-1965

Preface

When Ralph Mills proposed that I put together a selection of the reviews, interviews, literary, and personal essays I had written through the years, it was as if he had over-heard me thinking to myself. Mainly I have wanted to see these pieces bound together under one cover in order to study them as a whole for their relationship to those published poems I had written within the same years. Now that I have seen them together and read through them, I must admit to feeling already on the way to new grounds as I continue to write poems. It is in the poems that I do my hard thinking; while in the writing of re-views and essays, speaking for interviews, I have learned to articulate my thoughts in prose—after the fact of the poems. Such is probably the case for all writers who work at their craft. I simply hope that the reader will find what I have found here: at least an adequate account of the kind of poetry writing I have been doing until now, and the presentation, with some irregularity, of the ideas, insights, and opinions that went into the poems.

Some of the pieces were written to satisfy a need to write them at that moment, without thought of publish-ing them. They went into my desk drawers and were forgotten for years. Others were commissioned, such as reviews. Occasionally I have requested the opportunity to write a review about a particular book whose subject and style at that moment possessed me. It was all virtually unplanned, which I prefer. I would have bored myself otherwise, I'm sure. And I doubt that I would have started as a writer of nonfiction prose without the encouragement of the earliest and then most important mentor in my writing life, Lawrence Chauncey Woodman, dead now and buried in his home town in New Hampshire. He was an eccentric among the poets and writers of his day, but an inspired teacher. To him I owe much of my confidence and interest in my ability to write prose pieces. It was he who gave me the opportunity to write reviews for his small literary magazines, such as *American Scene, Literary Arts,* and others, all of which failed for lack of practical know-how nearly as quickly as he produced them on his mimeograph machine at home during the late thirties and early forties. I hope he hears all that I'm writing about him here. He died unhappy, feeling himself abandoned by his friends and followers. I did not abandon you, Lawrence. I had to go my way to write these pieces in solitude. Now they are here together, with interviews; and if your spirit is with us yet, I want it to know I dedicate this book to you.

David Ignatow

Editor's Note

The materials in this volume—essays, interviews, lectures, book reviews—were selected by the editor and David Ignatow; they include several unpublished pieces. Revisions and corrections have been made where it seemed necessary in the interests of clarity or to rectify minor errors. The arrangement of the work in sections II, III, and IV is in general chronological by publication date or by probable date of composition if a piece is unpublished. A date appears at the end of each item in the book. In section III, however, the articles are grouped topically, then chronologically; the book reviews follow in their original sequence. The prose of section IV resembles in some ways a mixture of qualities to be found in Ignatow's *Notebooks* and in some of his prose poems. These writings were difficult to date except by decade, though Ignatow has published one of these pieces very recently, I have retained the earlier dates after them. All in all, the various kinds of work gathered here provide a remarkably coherent impression of David Ignatow's background and experience, as well as his attitudes toward his life and art.

The editor wishes to acknowledge Mr. Scott Chisholm for the idea from which this book's title was derived and the assistance of Mrs. Frankie Warfield and other members of the secretarial staff of the English department at the University of Illinois at Chicago Circle in preparation of the manuscript for this book.

Ralph J. Mills, Jr.
University of Illinois
at Chicago Circle

Contents

I

The Beginning

At dinner, during the week, a dialogue on the family pamphlet bindery business would take place between my parents in the kitchen. On Saturday and Sunday evenings their dialogue would be carried on in the living room, there joined by guests, usually my uncle, my father's brother, and his wife. Clouds of smoke would roll from the cigars of the two men as they sat and talked before a radio playing music. I sat perched on the edge of the sofa and would alternately try to listen to the music and to the conversation. The year was 1927, I was a child attending elementary school, too young to be allowed out nights alone and so I made their interests mine. On weekends, the conversations were mild and studied in tone, partly in deference to the Sabbath, but mainly out of a wish to keep up a confident and calm appearance in front of company. It was during the week, when my father had only my mother to talk to, that the tensions of business were brought home, and late at night at that, after a long, hard day's work by my father. At the kitchen table, under the prodding of my mother's anxiety, he would start on his topic, at first grudgingly and slow. To him, it seemed impossible that anyone else could enter into his worries with the same emotional intensity. He had been wrapped in problems alone for so many hours.

My mother would sit hunched over the white porcelain tabletop across from him, her lips parted, waiting for the worst, as he chewed rapidly. Lifting his head for the moment, he would burst out with the news. It might be given angrily, depending upon the events that flooded back on him from the day. There seemed much to talk about, with something new to say each evening. To me, as a child, this outpouring was both terrifying and revealing. Nothing in the mechanics of arithmetic or spelling could compare to these nightly adventures with my parents. As I did my homework on the dining room table opposite the kitchen entrance, I would keep turning from my books to watch and listen, fascinated. They themselves would have forgotten everything else in their excited discourse, my father ignoring the taste of his food as it was chased down his throat in the rush to get out his words. My mother would be letting the soiled dishes in the sink wait to listen to him and join in with exclamations of anger or joy. Even as I sat alone in my room, studying with the door closed at a distance from the kitchen, a whole room beyond the dining room, their voices would penetrate feverishly. During the day I found myself anticipating my father's return home at night. My whole existence seemed to have become absorbed in following the fortunes of the family business.

There was school where I was being taught the principles of Americanism, among them being the right of each person to the pursuit of happiness. The teacher, a grown person like my parents, would stand before the class and lecture on the importance of the pursuit of happiness. It was not simply to be equated with money, clothing, and food. One could have them all in abundance and still not be happy. In the freedom of one's spirit one found happiness. On Friday mornings in the assembly hall the school principal would stand on his raised podium before the uplifted faces of his students to quote text: What did it avail a man to gain the whole world only thereby to lose his soul? I would go home, my head drumming enthusiastically with this new revelation, so opposite from what I had absorbed listening to my parents talk together. I would proclaim the difference to them as their salvation. Each night as they searched for happiness in the toils of business they only found themselves even more passionately enmeshed. Once I arrived home from school, however, I thought better of my project, nor did I venture to discuss it with them. Just to recall their feverish nights was to realize how entangled they were in their affairs. To remind them of better would only plunge them deeper into their despair and perhaps direct their anger at me. I decided to live silently, free of their cares and obsessions, as an example that they could follow, if they wished.

In this swing from the real to the ideal, from home to school, from my silent thoughts to the spoken thoughts of my parents, I graduated from elementary school and entered high school. Stimulated by an especially interesting course in history or English, I brought home text books issued at the beginning of the term, as well as books borrowed from the public library. I did not fully understand these books, nor hoped to soon, but their impact on me set me even further apart from my parents. The nightly talks between them still went on, now low and intense, now piercing and filled with angers. Subdued on weekends, it proved how sharp was their agony during the week. In time I began to write, in reaction to these ordeals, since to talk to my parents was out of the question. It would be unreal to them in their circumstances. To write was my only outlet. Eventually they would read my writing. The poetry of Walt Whitman prompted me, he who had swung so freely through the universe, who was so typically American in spirit, as I understood it from my school lessons and books. He had set behind him the narrow worldly cares to stride down the open road of the freedom of oneself. Like no one else, he stood for autonomy of the spirit. Body and soul together were celebrated in his poems. The spirit was of the flesh. One had only to turn to oneself for the reality. After graduation from high school, when my parents asked me to enter the family business, I refused.

I did not act on Whitman's proposition immediately. There still was the matter of getting a job. That was the alternative to refusing to enter the family business. Or else I had to leave home. My parents had neither the time nor the inclination to discuss the issues with me. I was shocked by their unilateral decision, particularly that of my father, but it went to prove the utter false-ness in which my family found itself, bound to business, divorced or isolated from the reality of one's true self. But I was not yet prepared to go out into the world, which conceivably could prove to be an even worse ex-perience, when I considered that my father was part of it. I thought of the strangers out there who had never heard of me and could care even less. The only real choice left to me, finally, was to enter the family business.

There I was confirmed in my thoughts about it. Free-dom of oneself was not to be found in business. Of that I was now certain. Not in the roar of machinery, nor in the harsh commands and flare-ups. These were unreal and sordid. They dragged me down. As a person I ex-pected consideration under any circumstance. My fa-ther's harsh, hysterical methods had not advanced him far in business either. Those nightly anxiety-ridden talks between my parents never ceased, and now they included me, my intransigence in the shop. For one, I refused to work longer hours than the ordinary worker in the shop and left promptly with the others at the end of the day. It was apparent to anyone there that my father's methods were failing with them, too. The shop was small and voices rising in anger and resentment could be heard constantly above the roar of the machinery. Wherever one looked was confusion and discord. Nothing could be worse than that in the outside world, I felt, my spirit was so depressed and bitter here. I had not expected anything quite like this, but given all that I had been taught and all that I had read, it was inconceivable to me that this and this alone was America. I would find a job to my liking, and be free. I decided to leave home too, since that was where my unhappiness began.

My search for a better life never quite succeeded. My demands were exacting. There were no jobs precisely like the one I expected to fill my requirements. I wanted a job where I could also sit back and think and feel the freedom within. It seemed a perfectly normal thing to do, according to my thinking, yet each job would have a way of negating that belief. It would create a conflict in me and between my superior and me that invariably would be resolved by my search for a new job. In time, it became a discouraging process, each job at first offering the possibility of ease and freedom, only to make itself felt as a burden and a threat to me. I began to realize that I was being confronted by an order of reality different from mine, that there were others who, like myself, also were in search of their personal freedom and happiness and were going about it in a manner entirely opposite from mine and from an entirely different set of premises. They were the men to whom I was responsible on the job, the supervisors and often the actual owners of the plant or office. I could not deny them the right that I gave myself, to form their lives according to their innermost wishes. It was a confusing insight to come upon, after my years of search for my own personal freedom. It somehow did not accord with the principles of Walt Whitman. Manhattan was where my search took place, and Brooklyn was my residence, where I was born and where my parents still resided in their two-family, red-brick house that conformed with all the others on the block.

As I tried to compromise and hedge as a last resort, to get over the rough spots, so to speak, it became obvious to me that I was bargaining away my freedom. One compromise would lead to another, as I acceded to that principle and saw it become a way of life. It was an unhappy dilemma to me, for by exercising my right to freedom I also was undermining my basis for it by depriving myself of the money and the leisure it afforded. I was filled with despair. Contrary to what I had been led to believe in school and in my favorite books, I could find no ground anywhere in which to root myself as a free man, and yet in the city I saw the huge crowds coming and going in streets, shops, and offices with the air of a people utterly unhampered in their lives. They looked and acted content and free and energetic, while I was without freedom, weighted down with gloom.

But there was refuge for me in my family. On each of my home visits I would receive a warm welcome, good food, and a relaxed hour or two. There was a tacit agreement between us to avoid the bristly issue of ideals. I was not yet prepared to acknowledge my defeat, not without arriving at some arrangement between us in which I could be comfortable with myself. We sought it in casual random conversation about living expenses and such prosaic problems for the single man on the outside world. My mother, however, could not long restrain herself and her shy, brusque manner would get to the thorny issue between us through a stratagem. It would be triggered by a polite inquiry by me on business conditions at the shop. She would promptly reply that business was good and that there was nothing any longer for anyone to worry about and get angry over. There was evidence enough of that in the house, the plump new sofa and chairs and plush rugs everywhere and a brand new expensive Oldsmobile parked in front of the house. My own failure was clearly evident in my silences and glum look, and shyly she would point out to me how everything in the shop now allowed for more ease and freedom for everyone, even the workers. She was deliberately oblique, as if to save me the embarrassment of having to assert my dignity again by rejecting an overt invitation to return. Her stratagem permitted me to think about her offer calmly as a solution indeed to my problem. She was the restless one between my parents. My father was satisfied with things as they stood. Success had come to him at last in nice measure and he could afford to sit back on a weekend, truly relaxed. She was not so easily compensated for the past, not until she could see me too share in the success. Usually these discussions between us would take place on a weekend, the tone calm and measured—more truthfully so than I could remember from those visits by my father's brother in the early days. There no longer was the undercurrent of anxiety, and so I felt there was a point to what she was hinting at. But by this time it no longer was a question for me of whether I could get along with others on my basis. I had no illusions about that basis now, and in any case it had to be subordinated to the overriding need to hold a job. I could see now, too, that being the son of the boss was valuable. It would be difficult, if not impossible, to fire me, but this time I would not leave in search of the impossible. To return, then, meant more than to further compromise myself. It was to give up my conception of personal freedom entirely. Several calm discussion-filled evenings subsequently helped me to make up my mind. Occasionally my father sat in on these talks, nodding approval of my mother's words. Nothing was left to make me hesitate. My poetry writing had begun to vanish amid the complications brought about by my endless search for personal freedom. In my writing I had tried to follow this commitment faithfully, only to find the words grow thin. They were becoming generalities, fading in the harsh rub of events, while those events had begun to lead me into other thoughts, decidedly unpleasant. I had begun turning to protest and satire in my poetry. It was, as I recognized, my way of stating that personal freedom was nonexistent. From there it was a simple step to enter the family business.

With it went no hope. There was nothing to take the place of what I had given up. For a while I had been living happily on a false assumption. The joy and bravery of it had been the whole of my life and now there was no happiness in giving it up. There was nothing but an admission that happiness did not exist. I felt no motive for living. One simply waited, slackened off, waited, and despaired, and found oneself not writing at all.

In the meanwhile I did have to make a living. Returned to my father's shop, I worked seriously and hard, forgetting myself in it. Eventually, under his guidance, I was given a position of authority. The bindery now was more than twice the size it had been when I left ten years before, and had more than twice the number of machines and workers. I was made production manager, in charge of scheduling and job specifications. It was grueling work. Among the other problems, customers had to be appeased for our failures to meet deliveries on schedule. In the shop, workers and their foreman had to be appealed to or, as it happened, threatened every step of the way if we were to live up to commitments. They would resent me and I would be embarrassed at having to prod them all through the day. Often enough as these commitments turned out to be impossible to fulfill, I would have to get on the phone and talk the customer into a new schedule or sit at the phone and take the abuse and anger of a man at the other end of the line frustrated in his own plans. It would enrage me to have to remain silent through his furious, humiliating harangue. The little that was left of me, now that I had returned defeated to the shop, was crushed altogether, and after hanging up I would stalk back into the factory and hysterically, like my father in the past, demand to know why our promises could not be kept and why it always had to be me who took abuse for broken promises for which other persons were responsible. The foreman and the workers would shrug their shoulders and look at each other, with disdain for me. It was the production man's job to take the blame, didn't I know? And if I became angry with them in earnest they would turn on me, with everyone else in the factory arrayed against me. My father would have to step out of the office and onto the factory floor where the argument was taking place and quiet the lot of us in his calm, authoritative voice and order us back to work again. I would be relieved but sullen, glad the heated words had been stopped before the workers and the foreman quit in a rising rage, and yet I would feel oppressed by a failure over which I had no control yet which had the power to give me this unwanted grief. I had felt no private commitment to my job and so had expected no personal blame or identity with it. Nevertheless, there remained the responsibility I had taken on with the job, of my own free will. I was caught.

During lunch, while chewing on a sandwich, I would

be huddled over the accounting books with my father, figuring out the profit and the loss. A day's work had to show a profit and there were days of long-run jobs when no profit was visible. These were the days hardest to bear. My father would be constantly on top of me, demanding facts and figures, and if he happened to be taking a hand in the production, soon tiring (he was growing old and feeble), he would be especially irritable and sharp. That was when I really had to hold my temper; that was the test of my attitude toward my job. After a few restrained words of clarification to placate him, through which I felt the tension mounting between us, I would walk away, ostensibly to overlook another part of the operation, but really to keep myself from blowing up and leaving. It was during these days that the tension would mount among the workers too. Their production would be under constant scrutiny by my father or myself, and a word of correction or advice would make a worker explode in anger and protest. I would have to stand there beside him silently, for fear of disrupting the schedule further by arguing back. Realizing how little all this meant to me in the way of happiness, it was a nightmare existence, and yet I had to go on with it with the passion and energy of a dedicated man. It was a bitterly ironic comment on my literary past to which I had given that same passion and energy.

After work, at home, the sullen faces of the workers kept entering my mind. Was it for this that I had searched for freedom and inner peace, to become a punishment to others?

I did not want to be alone in these thoughts; they made me feel so lost and abandoned in myself. I wanted to share my misery and self-hatred with others, to confess, to unburden myself, to be able to live with myself, if only on the marginal basis of confession. I began to spend the days in a kind of subterfuge for conversation with the workers. I would approach one with an order to do this or that and end by talking to him confidentially. How did he like this job, I would ask, with a wry twist to my voice which was meant to let him understand that I shared with him his distaste for it and his distaste for me who had to give him his orders. At first, he would look me over suspiciously, with a hurried side-glance as he worked, perhaps wondering whether I was looking for a pretext, out of his own mouth, to fire him. I would persist in my questioning, satirizing the whole place to him as an assurance that I was on his side. Out loud, as if addressing the questions to myself, I would wonder what caused any of us to work here? Were there no other shops where it might be easier or at least more congenial, closer to how one liked to live, in self-respect? The money was not enough to keep one here. Other shops offered money too. As I would continue in this vein he would begin to grin slowly and look at me directly. It was a kind of comment on my words. I was being naive in his eyes, if not downright childish. The questions were not worth answering. Here I was a boss who should know better than to ask questions that obviously answered themselves. We were both in the same game, so to speak, for the same thing. Wiping his hands thoroughly of the grease and grime, he prepared his words. He liked his job, he would say finally. He was glad to be doing it. All shops were alike. What was wrong with that? As for the money, what was wrong in having it? That's what kept him here and if he could get more of it he'd be even happier. He was under pressure to produce and that always called for more money, didn't it? And he looked at me challengingly, with a brief smile. I would be unable to answer and would walk away. I wanted to think quietly, alone. His remarks would set me back. I would be stunned by the attitude behind them. He fully accepted his life, with its hardships and complications. He would have more of it, on yet a bigger scale, with more tension thrust on him, providing it assured him more money. In fact, it was as if he was notifying me that he meant to have it. My speaking to him on this confidential level had given him the opportunity which he may have been looking for all the while to hit me for a raise. I was confused.

During the same week, again under the subterfuge of checking on production schedules, I went from worker to worker, wanting to find out if each had this same attitude. All did, without exception. All were emphatic on the single point of more money, regardless that it meant increased work for them. They were making no distinction between themselves and the boss. He too was out for money and so they demanded their share. The theory that they were being exploited had no basis in reality with them. The only purpose of having bosses was to gain money through them. My guilt and fears in my relationship to them were a myth, as far as they were concerned, and I began to sense my childishness toward them for having confronted them with such an issue as personal happiness and freedom. They had solved those problems by immersion in money. During my questioning they had looked at me with surprise and suspicion as though suspecting my motives as perhaps seeking ways and means of getting more work out of them for less money, but they had made sure of squashing that thought by demanding more. I walked away from each conversation, always baffled and let down. Their attitude seemed incredible in the face of the hardships they had to put up with in this shop. What did they expect money would do for them? After a day's work, they were exhausted from the pounding noise of the machines and from the constant handling of materials that they placed on the machines and that emerged as finished products with the regularity of a clock. They had no respite from their work, except for the brief lunchtime. The next morning they would return, sullen and grumbling, anticipating what was in store for them that day. I could hardly question anyone in the morning or hand him a schedule of required production for that day without getting in exchange a sullen look or rough answer. That was what their labor produced in them and so what more could they expect from it by an infusion of more money? They already had their refrigerators, cars, television sets, and washing machines and many among them owned their homes and cars. Yet they would come to work each morning just as determined to resist and be sullen as if they had none of these precious possessions. These were the pride and joy of their labors, judging from the way they spoke about them during lunchtime. Sullen and grunting in the morning, they would sound off against the job with the free manner of a person of independent means and yet they were all bound to this shop, and would be to any shop for that matter, by household debts, mortgages, weekly bills, time payments, and ultimately by this overall belief that there was nothing else worthwhile to take the place of making money.

How then could they reconcile their passion for money with the agonies it put them through? If life was meant to be lived in the comforts with which they surrounded themselves at home, if it was possible, according to their beliefs, to call that happiness, then was not this factory, its tension and pressure to produce, its irritations and physical exhaustion, the very opposite of what they believed in and lived for? How were they able to tolerate it? I went around again to talk to each, probing. Were they really content with their jobs? Was it the kind of life they had planned for themselves? Was there nothing else they had dreamed, better than this angry, tiring work? I could not put these questions directly, in my position as production manager. It was during lunchtime as they all sat around a big worktable and ate their home-made sandwiches and talked that I was able to bring up the subject, but only obliquely, by referring to an item in the newspaper as basis for comment, or perhaps some incident in the shop which had caught everyone's attention, personal and plain to see, as for example, the not unusual incident of a worker suddenly expressing his disgust with the job and shutting down the machine to walk off to the toilet to smoke awhile and recover his composure before returning to the shop. It was all right, the others grinned at each other, but it was a bad habit and shouldn't be repeated too often. One could get fired. As unhappy as they were at their work, they were fixed in it. I tried to understand that. They had grown up expecting nothing else out of life. They discussed their lives with the same detachment that they ran their machines. It had been given to them to live this way from the start. They had had no hand in shaping it. It was not that they were voicing their resentment or rebellion. They were simply stating the facts, and the facts were a kind of symbol among them of what they shared in common with each other. It allowed them to go on to discuss other matters of more immediate concern about which they could talk more meaningfully, such as refrigerators, television sets, and washing machines. They talked with enthusiasm, quoting price and make by heart of nearly all models. They had their newspapers to refer to at once for corroboration and they would spread them out on the worktable as they ate and point at items listed by the dozens, page after page. They would carry their newspapers underarm as they entered the factory and as they left each night. This was how they survived the day and got along. To me, it offered no explanation other than to see in it their confession of helplessness to do other than what they were doing and their readiness to do it, to exploit themselves like any boss.

It was harrowing to see them in that light and yet it was a life they accepted. They found good in it. When they did rebel, shutting down a machine to walk off to the toilet, they would come back, having temporarily modified their enslavement and affirmed themselves thereby, but to question their cars, houses, and refrigerators—these were the untouchables, the sacred, without which life itself did not exist for them. These were not to be questioned. Like themselves, they saw the boss too being driven, to make the business pay off his costs and earn him a still better car than theirs. He had his special problems to face, competition from other bosses, overhead, fixed expenses. They could sense that the world also was a vast, impersonal machine for which no one actually was responsible, not even the boss, whom they respected for his ability to make the machine work for him and give them work in return. He deserved his better car and larger, more elaborately furnished home, with perhaps a maid or two, but they could be angry with him when he lost out to a competitor on the price bid for a job. How often they would protest at a loss in their earnings during a slow week. He was there, they felt, to see that they earned a living as he did from their labors and he was not exempt from blame if he was losing out to the competition, just as they were not exempt from blame when they did not live up to their production schedules. It was a circle of mutual accommodation, they felt, in which all were joined and for which all were responsible in keeping it intact and healthy. To try to break this circle was like trying to destroy their own welfare and happiness. How often they would sit around the lunchtable to compare notes on wages in different shops to note the advantage or disadvantage to themselves. And how angry they would become to learn that another shop was offering more work. They would make clear to me or to my father their anger and counter our defense with arguments of their own just as reasonable sounding as ours, such as their willingness to work longer hours, if necessary, to keep a job in the shop, a job that we might have lost temporarily or permanently because of a lack of time to produce it. When we would hesitate to take on a job that showed a very slim margin of profit, they would search out working methods that could produce more at less cost. These were methods that would make them work even harder, making it that much more difficult for them to break away from the machine for a smoke in the toilet. So it went each day, with one side egging on the other to greater and greater exertions. It was a life lived in earnest.

I, thinking about all this and feeling as helpless as the workers, saw it as an era like any other, with its central obsessive icon dignified through suffering. It was our means to salvation. We could not do other than what we had been formed to do and so had raised that necessity to a faith.

I went home to write poetry again in this vision, tragic for its revelation of the kind of happiness it embraced. It was not what I had sought at the beginning. That had been foolhardy and even dangerous to life. One sought happiness through self-surrender. And so there was poetry to be written, about this paradox of the perpetual search for personal happiness and freedom in things other than oneself.

1950-76

II

Interviews

An Interview

With Scott Chisholm

*Mr. Ignatow, you are widely known as a poet of the city—
a poet, according to one critic, "condemned to be a resi-
dent." Does this association have any aesthetic meaning
for you? And if it does, would you discuss the effect it
has had upon your conception of poetry?*

Well, let me try to give you some background. I was
brought up in Brooklyn which had some sort of subur-
ban atmosphere to it. I didn't know too much about
the city for a good many years—in fact, not before I was
about fourteen or fifteen when I began to travel in to
New York. Even then it was some sort of grotesque thing
to me, although very fascinating.

I think of city life as the only sort of life that's rele-
vant for personal issues. Living in Brooklyn was a way of
sleeping your life away. I thought of Brooklyn as that
great part of America that lived under the trees and
among the grasses, knowing that something else was
happening in other areas, especially New York. You had
to have New York on the mind.

At the age of eighteen, I left Brooklyn and went to
New York. That gave me some idea of what New York
was all about, and living in New York I assumed it was
the only place where you could really think about hu-

man relationships—something which you found lacking in Brooklyn. Human relationships weren't going on in Brooklyn. They were generally routines of eating, sleeping, and making a living. But in New York you met people at various places and had ideas to talk about. So I'd say the aesthetics of New York became the aesthetics of my poetry.

You asked me if I could discuss the effects it had on my conception of poetry. Well, to begin with, I wasn't the least bit interested in writing a poetry of New York. In fact, some of the critics will be surprised when my new book (*Poems 1934-1969* [1970]) comes out—surprised to see how many love poems were written just before my involvement with New York and before I became conscious of what New York was doing to the world outside and to itself.

Writing that sort of New York poetry became a deliberate choice when I found that living in New York and writing romantically wasn't quite the thing to satisfy me. New York was romantic on a different level. It was romantic in a very ugly way. Ugliness was ugly only in perspective—that is, from a perspective of the past. But living through the life of New York meant living your own life. It wasn't fair to yourself to call it ugly. But because the influence of the past was so strong while writing in the present, you may have had compunctions about the truth. Looking back upon the truth, you see it as beautiful.

Your early work was once rejected because of what one critic called "flat rhythms" and for a "language of personal suffering which had none of the literary pleasures of style to relieve it." But in reviewing Say Pardon, *the same critic saw "a new impetus in Ignatow's language," which he likened to a softening of words "taking plea-*

sure in themselves." Isn't it perhaps true that the images of the city which compelled you to write in the first place overpowered the poet's language in your very early work?

No. It was done deliberately as I began to sense the demands of the city poem. I had to meet the city on its own terms if I was going to get it into my work. That meant being overwhelmed by the city's life in order to emerge with all the facts. This is how language becomes transformed from one historical period to the next, through history or the individual. I was not going to write in the iambic pentameter when the very tone and pace of the city denied such a regular, predictable, and comfortable style—comfortable, of course, from long use and its acceptance as style. I wanted the spirit of the city in my poems while I, as a city man, knew how to manipulate the spirit in terms of its language. I was the city's artist and as its artist I could feel both in and out of the city at the same time.

You've written, I believe, of guilt as the link between the poet and his world. "Guilt," you write in Say Pardon, *"is my one attachment to reality." Is this the moving force behind your work? I sense it in all the poems about your father.*

Well, my father is one element in the work, and guilt is a sense I derive from society itself. I think the whole society is laboring under a sense of predestined guilt. We're Puritan. No matter how you turn it or how you phrase it, we're guilty for cultural reasons—or lack of reasons which the culture withholds from us.

I'd say, of course, that guilt is the one driving factor in my work. I am guilty, by all standards of ideal behavior and modes of existence, of falling far short of their demands. Of course I'm guilty—like everyone else. It's a guilt I live with, although in my daily life I try hard to act with some kindliness, ease, and love for my fellow man. I try hard to put it into practice, even if it makes me out to be a slow-thinking fool. I'm really working hard within to repress my hostility, my aggressive desire to dominate and direct, and my love to hurt others. I'm American. It's all in the poems.

The tension, however, ends there and I use it to defuse the guilt in poems that have as their reference another and more ideal form of conduct. Therefore, you might say the guilt is there to manifest another ideal which we're falling short of. That is the whole point of the guilt—whether or not I use it personally.

Of course, I use myself personally. It's a technique that we Americans are using with Walt Whitman as a model. We've been following Walt Whitman in this path—except that we reinvent Whitman's ideals today and try to point to their failure. As individuals, we still use ourselves as the metaphors, as he did the metaphors of hope and faith. We use ourselves now as the metaphors of failure of the American ideals.

Would you say that Whitman exerted more of an influence on your earlier work than he did on your later work? I'm thinking of this with particular reference to William Carlos Williams as a later influence.

I would say, yes, that I was naively accepting Whitman on his own terms until I began to see the world in modern terms. The bitterness or the disillusionment, which I experienced personally, forced me to invert all that Whitman had to say and to disprove the sense of brotherhood that he thought we had among us—disprove the love of life that he thought we had among us—disprove every item of his ideal about American progress and America as the Faith of the Nations. We are some nation to look to, aren't we, at this point?

This is the bitterness. This is Whitman still exerting an influence on American poetry. Unquestionably, he still is. He remains the important factor to whom we must address ourselves. We address ourselves as sons to a father who finds his sons no longer believing in what he has to say, but who are taking, point for point, everything he had to say and showing how it is the opposite of what he thought or hoped for.

I sense something of this denial of Whitman in my next question. Some critics have found a quality in your poetry in which "emptiness, by some strange reversal, has become spiritual." In Figures of the Human *you have a poem which begins, "The song is to emptiness." Are you aware of this aspect of your poetry?*

Yes. I've felt that about my work. It's the emptiness of consolation. How do we console ourselves in a world that can no longer be motivated by the ideals of the nineteenth century? We haven't any ideals to speak of now and the spirituality is the sense of defeat. For us it's a defeat that forces us into a kind of humbleness.

I don't dare say that it's become a religious thing. It's not quite that at all. No, one can acknowledge one's shortcomings without having to make some sort of prayer to an unknown god. It's not necessary. In that sense, I guess I'm a stoic.

In reading many of the confessional poets, one gets the feeling that the stuff dug from the ground of personal experience is really intended as an implied answer. A great deal of your work, however, is literally questions. Poems like "How Come?," "Figures of the Human," and "Get the Gasworks" are filled with them. Is this resistance to making answers from experience, or perhaps to answers at all, at the root of the frustration which fills your poems?

No, I don't think this is a resistance to answers from experience. In fact, in my questions I'm forcing the issue. I'm seeking to force people to see what reality is. It's a polemical technique.

It's not intended to avoid answers from reality. It was intended to pinpoint, to converge, to force the reader to converge upon reality and to focus upon it so much more sharply because it's a question that's intended to startle him. At least, I thought in those terms. Whether it actually comes out that way in the art, I don't know. It makes a very good question.

Would you say that in a poem like "How Come?" the title is, in a sense, the whole point?

Are you referring to the poem about the soap?

Yes, that's the one. I believe it begins Say Pardon.

Well, it's not an evasion. I'm really satirizing the whole reality—which is sudsy. I'm saying that if you take all this seriously, then you have my questions to burst your bubbles, if you have any sense of humor at all about yourself. If you're a New Yorker, you certainly will get the drift of it and laugh at yourself. You'll know that you're being kidded and teased.

Then one of the things that is necessary to the meaning of your work is a sense of humor.

Yes. Yes. That is, if you don't want to do the next worse thing, which is to go jump off the dock.

One of your critics talks about a suicide wish in Figures of the Human. *Possibly your worst critic claims that you are possessed by what he calls "an habitual nightmare of unprovoked and lethal assault." Twenty-nine of those poems, he claims, are concerned with violence. Most of the images involve either knives or knifings. What is your interest in violence in your poems? Is the knife a part of the larger symbolic intention of your work?*

What is my interest in the images of violence in my poems? Well, what is the interest of this whole country in violence? Historically, we were born in violence. We create in violence. We kill in violence. If this critic thinks of violence in my work as a pejorative thing, he's perhaps ignoring what we know about the country we live in. I'm dealing personally with violence because I think of myself as a metaphor for the whole society. The way I see American society, the individual is at the center of his culture. That's forced upon him. The Puritan demand for a man to fulfill himself and justify himself to his God—supposedly God—or to his community, forces upon man the whole cultural burden of upholding the ethos of his time; therefore, he's at the center.

A poet, therefore, is justified in making himself the metaphor of his community. If violence is the great and important image in his work, it's only because it's been proven to be the one overriding experience we have had in this country and which we will probably continue to have—a sense of violence about ourselves. Our subways are violent. Our trucks are violent. Our traffic is violent. I show what violence comes to. I hope, in my poetry, I show what it comes to.

Do you sense in this criticism of your work an indication that the critic, to be able to make that statement, does not have a very real conception of the world—your world?

I think I know who the critic was and there's no point in mentioning his name. The fact is that he has a certain bias toward poetry that is, from my point of view, all right for a lyrical poet who has himself to deal with, facing a mirror or living in a room that's permanently sealed against noise—except, of course, for the echoes of his own voice.

My kind of writing forces me to go out among people. I'm not a social poet. I'm a poet of individuality and I only know my individuality by interacting with others. I can't do less than respond as I'm made to respond by environment. Yet I'm conscious, as a poet, of exactly what's happened to me. So there are these two levels— one on which I have to do what's happening to me, and one on which I know what's happening to me. Poetry is intended as a dimension which might make me independent, in some ways, of my life, but only insofar as I'm aware of what's happening. It's not any more or less than what Wallace Stevens was saying in his theory of poetry. The reality is what you live with: the imagination is what you do with reality. The imagination gives the meaning to your experiences. The meaning to my experience is in the poems about the knifings I have seen and that I have read about and that I know are all around me.

Much of this is evident from those poems which you preface with material taken from newspapers.

Yes.

Let's return, for the moment, to the critic you were just

mentioning. He was the one who reacted against your use of the words chicken guts *in one of your poems. He made you out to be the poetic equivalent of a cinema tough guy, like Bogart—perhaps without any understanding.*

I think he simply didn't understand. In fact, he couldn't possibly with the sort of sensibility he brings to my work. It's a sensibility that is cultivated with academic honors and is beautifully aligned with the past. It's very much indebted to the past.

From this point, the past as we see it is quite dead and wouldn't be disturbing to anyone reading of the past. So coming upon the present, for a sensibility of this sort, is more than upsetting. It's a kind of reality that has never been experienced by that kind of sensibility and which will always be rejected.

In your recent review of James Wright's Shall We Gather at the River, *you spoke of the questions "his anguish asks" and you called his book "a metaphor of our land." To read those poems, you implied, is to get into "a mainstream of American consciousness." Your own poems as they concern the city—some as they concern the war—are equally metaphorical in their anguish. Do you see this anguish in the mainstream as bringing together any group of poets?*

Most of us are in that mainstream. For example, I had a very good chat with Gary Snyder over lunch one day last week. We talked about what the Vietnam war was doing to the people of this country—what it was doing to the poets.

Gary and I come from very different backgrounds. He's a farm guy, brought up on a farm, and he remained in California most of his life. The "wide open spaces" are very appealing to him. He loves the mountains, the woods. I was brought up in the city. I know the city the way he knows the mountains and the woods.

We met on the common grounds of anguish—the feeling that we were being deprived of our heritage through the war; that the country itself was slipping away from us into bestiality. That's the feeling we both have, and we agree on this. So if Gary and I, who are so far apart in our upbringing, have this in common, I can't think of how poets here and now could disagree about anguish being the important thing we are now living through.

I knew when I was writing the Wright review that I was not speaking only for Wright, but I was in some ways speaking over his head and addressing my remarks to readers in general and to other poets—letting them know how much we had in common with one another. Here was Wright doing a superb job of it. It was like a call to protest, a call to arms, a call to nonviolent demonstration. That's really what I was trying to say.

One of the things connected with the sense of anguish in modern life is the concept of alienation which has been used to describe the predicament of modern man. But alienation, even as a concept, has become a cliché. Is there an alternative to the cliché, another way of stating it from a poetic standpoint?

Yes, I agree it's become a cliché. But the generation that is coming up now—the students—this generation is just beautiful in its struggle to identify with the ideals of the country. They have completely disregarded the concept of alienation. They say that if anyone is alienated, it is the group in power that is alienated from American ideals. They are the "minority," whereas the mainstream is still fighting for America to realize itself. The students are in the forefront of this struggle.

So the emphasis has changed. It seems to me that it has changed. These students believe that they are Americans in every sense of the word and they want to impress this upon so-called power groups to let them recognize in themselves that they have lost their own way—that they've lost their way from what America means.

One of the oversimplifications that has been applied to your work is that you've been alienated. But I think you would admit that even though you write out of a sense of anguish, you are not the least alienated from New Yorkers or from the poetry of the city.

No. I feel no alienation as far as the city goes. I feel closer to the city than to anything else, only because a city to me is a world in small—especially New York.

I had the opportunity to teach out West and I was offered another job in the Midwest. I had these choices and I rejected them because to me New York is where I owe a debt of thanks. I must prove in some way that I can be of help. Where I was given help, I would like to return that favor in kind. In other words, I decided to teach here in New York and teach students who are finding it very difficult to get ahead.

Do you think that a poet like Robert Bly, for example, does something of the same kind for the Midwest?

Yes. Yes. That's why I'm really so admiring of Robert, and, really, this is what I feel we have in common. We've got to do something for our own area. We can't simply go away, taking with us what it gave us and leaving nothing in return.

I don't sense anything in Bly's poetry, either, of alienation from the Midwest, but I think there's a distinction that has to be made between the poetry of protest and the poetry of alienation.

Yes. The poetry of protest arises from the very fact that a person identifies with this environment, and he's horrified to find not that it's turning against him, but it's turning against itself. This is really what's causing the protest. It's as plain and simple as that.

I want to return to the Wright review. In that review you made this comment: "A poet who can write with the freshness of his grief has given himself the joy of his identity." In many of your poems, including those about your father, there is much grief, but little joy of identity. The revelations are like sand in the eyes. In writing that comment on Wright, were you thinking about yourself? Or have you excluded yourself from that joy?

No! I think the joy is in making the truth known. I think I should continue to write about my father, who I understand much more clearly now than I did then, and that's only because I've been able to find myself on a plateau of my own achievement where I can look around me with some kind of relaxation and see that he wasn't the ogre I made him out to be. He was just another man under terrible stress who needed time and help to realize his own responsibilities, of which I was one. But he had to ask me to help him, and I still wasn't able to realize that he needed my help. I was, as the child, looking for help from him. So that has passed, and I can see where I need to do something about it to straighten the record.

In writing about the problems we had together, I got a great kick in putting him down exactly as I thought he was—exactly the feelings as I was experiencing them at the time. So the pleasure is in the writing and if it's not obvious in the reading, then, it's because you're not me.

In his essay on Rescue the Dead, *Robert Bly praises the title poem, which contains the line, "Not to love is to live." He views it as a significant departure from a "tradition of popular opposites" which he identifies as the tradition of Auden and Lowell. Do you agree with his assessment? Was it part of your intention?*

Well, Robert says that I was using it as a significant departure from a tradition of popular opposites—the tradition of Auden and Lowell. I wasn't conscious of that, of creating this opposite. I was just working again out of personal experience and trying to enlarge it for a wide audience.

I suppose, looking back upon the poem, I would say that you could take that line too literally—"Not to love is to live." It's quite bitter in the sense that I think that living under these terms would be a kind of death in life.

But how do you live without love? You live, I guess, mechanically or financially, but you don't really live without love. In the last analysis, you love yourself, which is manifested in the fact that you continue to live.

So I think Robert is taking this point just a little too literally. I don't say that love is all. No, by no means, no. I'm saying that the problems that love will force upon you are the problems of living, and if love is the one fact to which you owe your life and your happiness, then I think you're in a bind. This is what I'm saying. You're in a bind. You don't live a life of love here and now. It's impossible. You don't do it. It never was done. So you live a sort of temporizing kind of existence. I'm quite clear about that in the ending of the poem when I say, "You who are free,/rescue the dead." By free, I mean those who can live or think they can live without love.

But I'm offering that as an irony at the same time. Having gone through the poem stage by stage showing what it is to live without love and then to return to those who are living through love and in love, I turn back to those who think they are living without love and ask them to save us who are under the influence of love. It would be quite obvious from what I have said about living without love that they who would help us must first help themselves.

You mentioned the temporizing quality of love in our society—which leads me to this question. Bly says that your poem "Rescue the Dead" involves the recognition that "nine-tenths of our love is ordered love, love we undertake at the demand of civilization, idealistic love."

Love itself is a form of faithfulness, but to seek faithfulness in love itself is to create an artificial standard—a center which doesn't exist. If love no longer exists, that's not the fault of love. It's not because we're not faithful; it's because love has lost its basis. So the students are right. The younger generation is right in saying that love is an absolute in itself. But if it's put to the uses of society, it becomes a living death. It isn't allowed free of social demands. That's the problem. It's true. I agree in that sense, but I don't know whether this is what's attracting the students. I can't say. I'm not sure. I can only speak personally again. When Robert says that "nine-tenths of our love is ordered love, love we undertake at the demand of civilization," he is right. But what does he mean by *idealistic* love? Or to put it another way, how does he define love? These are questions I would want to put to him.

Don't you sense in Bly's use of that word a meaning which refers to pop love—or cinema love?

That would be the definition of idealistic love?

Yes. That's what I was thinking. Perhaps he was getting at that.

In that sense, yes, I would agree with him. But I think then what he should have said was *idealized* love.

That might have been a better word. I sense in the poems you have written for your wife a love that is not idealized—a human love. Is this the type of poem which you wrote perhaps as a reaction to the baseness which idealized love has produced in our society?

That's right. Yes, that's right. I can't start rewriting the poems and talk to you about them, but you said it correctly for me. It's the human factor in love that gives love its attractiveness. It's full of unpredictable ways, and needing it, we are in constant search of it. Very often we lose it—very often. Just as often we recover it, but in the recovery comes the great thrill—that we are capable of recovering that which we lost.

Do you think it is possible for readers of your poetry to see a stark contrast between the poems which you have written for your wife and those written about the city?

There is a contrast and I meant it in the sense that the possibility for a relationship between two persons exists in society where people make an effort to live with one another, to understand, and to help and support one another. This is one product of love. This is what sets us apart from society as a whole. I suppose that sort of love is possible among most people, and probably is something that is happening all the time. It's quite possible. But it does withdraw you from the competitive spirit in society—the competitive spirit that even invades our public ideas of love.

Your wife, Rose Graubart, was the artist who designed the jacket covers for Rescue the Dead *and* Figures of the Human. *I sensed a unity between the design and the poetry before I knew who she was. I suppose you sense that unity too?*

Yes. My wife has been working steadily at her art ever since our marriage, which goes back more than thirty years, and her influence on my work has been extraordinary. I suppose it has happened the other way around also. We have worked together on many ideas and very often, over lunch or dinner, we talk about the work we're doing. Her criticism and suggestions I take back with me, just as she, in showing me her drawings and paintings, is happy to hear my constructive comments.

 The fact that she is doing so many sketches of poets is a reflection of the kind of life we lead together. It's quite unified: it's quite harmonious in that sense, although it's not as even as life can be, given easier temperaments. We're both not easy temperaments.

Let's switch for a moment from readers to poets. I remember a remark by Louis Simpson in a special issue of The Nation *in which he states that he can see "very little similarity between the aesthetic principles of James Wright and Allen Ginsberg, or Robert Creeley and W. S. Merwin, or Robert Bly and Gary Snyder." He seems to think that these poets could only agree on what they dislike. Do you see his comment as valid?*

The way it's quoted to me, I would say he hasn't looked at it very closely. We all share the same techniques. In fact, when a generation has done its work and the next generation looks back upon those poets, it's seen almost at once that they've interacted with one another poetically. The work, for example, of Verlaine and Baudelaire and Rimbaud share many techniques in common. They were all of the same period. The work of Shakespeare, Beaumont, and Fletcher, and Ben Jonson and Webster have so much in common, yet the differences are obvious because of differences of personality and differences of temperament.

I know that James Wright uses surrealism in conjunction with objective observation. He manages to work the two together, as I said in my review, and he gives the whole thing a new force. The two modes help one another. They seem to do something for one another, these two different methods. Now that's an example of a poet who's taking from two schools and creating a school of his own, if you want to put it that way. So Simpson, in saying that there isn't enough in common aesthetically between the poets he has named is not really precise, not really looking at the facts.

What about his statement that they could only agree on what they dislike?

That's what I'm refuting, from my point of view. I think they have a good deal in common. I guess one poet emphasizes one method more than another, but they do share methods. The way Creeley breaks the line is the way Robert Bly breaks the line—for almost the same reason. But he doesn't call it a *voice*; he has an *imagistic* explanation for it. You could read a Robert Bly poem the way you read a Robert Creeley poem and there would be no harm in it. In fact, it might do something for the Bly poem. You might see it from a different angle.

It's also quite possible to see in Creeley certain surrealist elements—the kind of surrealist elements that Robert Bly uses. There are poems by Creeley—I can't quote them now, but I know his work—in which he uses the techniques of arbitrary imagery at the root of surrealism. I've seen enough of his work to say this. Unfortunately, I don't have any of his poetry with me here. In the same way, Gary Snyder and Robert Bly have a lot in common. For one thing, they're constantly dealing with nature. Snyder, of course, has a different emphasis. Bly's emphasis on nature is kind of mythopoetic, whereas Gary's is quite natural and distinctly the thing in itself. As for techniques, well, they both are presentational. For instance, you could say that Robert Bly has a good deal in common with W. S. Merwin, who is absolutely a surrealist-fantasist poet. And Bly's making every effort to create an archetypal poetry.

So I'm not going along with what Simpson says at all. I see elements of agreement in each. The emphasis is the important thing; they share techniques in common. All of them do.

This leads naturally to my next question. How is your own aesthetic similar or different from what you see operating in the poets whom Simpson mentions?

I can't be that conscious about my own work. I know I do surrealist work when I have to, and I know I write straight from observation when I have to—or I write lyrically in open vowels, or very frequently the way Jim Wright likes to write. And I write enigmatically or epigrammatically as Simpson likes to write—the short four line poem that punches an idea across. I've also seen myself do the very mysterious thing that W. S. Merwin does.

In other words, I have committed myself to a complete range of techniques. If anyone is an example to refute what Simpson is saying, I would put *myself* in that position. That is, I've used all those techniques and I continue to use them. In fact, there are poems where I combine all of them at once.

So I'm not saying that I have anything different from the others. All I'm saying is that the emphasis is where the difference takes place. That's where Simpson would agree, and I would welcome his opinion. It's not the technique; it's the emphasis on different techniques which creates a certain tone to the work—a different direction.

Simpson also says that American poets have joined in a common revulsion against the war in Vietnam, which they are "nearly all agreed to dislike." He views this reaction as not likely to produce good poetry in the short run, but something which "may serve to change the poets profoundly, so that in future their poems will be political in a way that really counts—that is, by altering their angle of vision." Would you agree? You edited the issue of Chelsea *in 1960 that anticipated the new political involvement of poetry and prose.*

I don't agree with Simpson's stand. I've only to think of a couple of poems by Robert Bly—two would be enough—to make evident this major change in American poetry. A real and very new dimension has been added, if only with those two poems. Now there's a new one that Bly has written—a very long one—which I expect will be published very shortly. It's very powerful and crushing.

Why can't Jeremiah come back to live again? Why can't he tell us where the problems are? And where is Isaiah? Is there only one Isaiah? That's not so. It can't be.

Which poems of Bly's are you thinking about specifically?

"Counting the Small-Boned Bodies," for one. "Johnson's Cabinet Watched by Ants," for another. I think I can say it modestly enough that I've written a couple of good ones myself. What's more, I think that Simpson, despite his protest, has written a couple of good ones also, which can stand up to poems with traditional themes. Antiwar poems have been written ever since man's mind began to think.

What about the "angle of vision" which Simpson talks about? In your own work, for example, poems like "All Quiet," "An American Parable," and "A Meditation on Violence" indicate a new vision, one which gets you beyond the images of the city. Is this a change you welcome?

If this is a change, it's only a change of venue. I don't know whether I've said it, but the city is to me the nature of reality today. Wars spring from cities. I don't know how to explain it, but the concentration of population where everything is happening—the whole political crux, the crucible in American life—is the city. That's where things are formed; that's where ideas are formed. Impulses are given structure and driven home.

If there is a war, as there is a war now [1970], it has to go with the nature of our reality, and that is centered in our cities. So when I write against a war, I'm really talking about the whole business of living in America.

The whole Vietnam war is really an extension of American life, of city life, of city living, and of our conception of life as it flows from this. We have a missionary quality also; we think we have to live in such a way as to create for ourselves a paradise to which others will come and be grateful—very grateful—for having it. But by the same token, we say that certain ethnic groups aren't up to the missionary spirit that Americans have. So we lend them a hand, or *force* them by hand to come our way. Anyone with a missionary spirit will go so far as to use force, if necessary, because if he's that much convinced of his own right, he will have to do something about it to realize it. We do this. So in talking about the war, it's not so much going beyond the city. I'm not going beyond it. I'm trying to show how it also applies to another form of life that we're going through. We think we're fighting an idealistic war. We're not. We're fighting a war that, in its very nature, is just as corrupt, despoiled, and brutal as the kind of lives we're forced to lead among ourselves at home—purely an extension of our existence here. I'm just using the idea of war as another expression of the same thing.

What do you think about Simpson's remark about the Olson school as "a system of breathing and using the typewriter that will enable anyone to write poetry naturally, without thinking"?

It's pretty funny. Taken out of historical perspective, the remark is amusing and makes a point. But I like to give Olson some credit for freeing poets from the bonds of the 1950s sleepy kind of writing that was going on at the time.

I, for one, don't write that way—using "a system of breathing." I know others who do, and when they do, I ask them whether my breathing can fit into their kind of breathing and we try to breathe together. I find, occasionally, that my breath is a little shorter than theirs, so I have to stop. You know.

So as a principle, I think the Olson thing is somehow

specious. As an impulse toward freedom—as a method of breaking away from what was going on in the 1950s when it was first enunciated—it's fine; it's O.K. It helped. It did something to help break away.

Do you think Ginsberg is a great breather?

Ginsberg has been a great poet. I could read him any way—short, long, fast, or slow. It all comes out the same for me.

Much has been written of your connection with the poetry of William Carlos Williams. You've mentioned it today. In fact, one of your more important essays for Chelsea *is a discussion of the social significance of his work—especially* Paterson, *which you see as a reaction to Eliot's clericalism and detachment from the social scene. Like Williams's, your own work is anything but detached. It finds its grist in fumes and street noise; in office workers, managers, and salesmen—a society both urban and suffering. What is your personal debt to Williams?*

Well, I think his work gave me the courage to do my own thing about the city. I felt liberated in being completely free in my so-called prose rhythms. I dared myself to write the free, natural language—and in writing it, I had Williams's work to support me.

So I would say that the first poet who put me onto the colloquial speech of our times on which I base most of my work, even today, was William Carlos Williams. This is a lasting debt that I owe him. Other than that, we are very different poets, and yet I was freed by him to do my own work.

Briefly, what do you see as the essential difference between yourself and Williams?

I've done it in poetry and it's pretty hard to say, at this point. I suppose the difference is that I felt the absolute hopelessness in things as they are, and this hopelessness manifested itself in my poetry; whereas Williams, seeing how low a state we had come to in this country, had some residue of hope centered in the individual—that we could reform ourselves and create anew our society closer to American ideals.

I don't think that's possible. I think that the coming changes will simply be unrecognizable from Williams's point of view. As a matter of fact, they've already happened.

In my essay on the influences of William Carlos Williams, I pointed out how Ginsberg completely destroyed any basis for hope in American society as it was constituted—centered in the individual; laughed at or destroyed or tore apart satirically all the hopes and energy that Williams reflected in his work. My own work, in its way, has said the same thing as Ginsberg's.

I think if Williams had continued to live and continued to see what we are going through now—I think—no. You can't speak for the dead—you can't. But the way his work was going, and in the direction it was going, I believe he would have wanted to agree with us. Whatever faith he had in America as a people would have to be completely reconsidered in view of the political and historical changes that we are now experiencing.

You're coming out early in 1970 with an edition of poems—a collected edition. What has been your intention in this volume and how have you ordered or arranged it?

We are taking all the poems that I consider good and worth republishing from the five previous volumes, and to these we have added about 150 new poems—poems from three decades, poems that have been lying in my drawer pretty much untouched for one reason or another, poems from the 1930s, the 1940s, the 1950s, and some from the early 1960s which I wrote and just put away.

Looking back upon them, I was able to see that those unpublished poems of the 1930s held up as poems and had points for now. It was the same with the poems of the 1940s. I think they're pretty good. At least, I had that reaction from others who read them before I made up my mind—others like Robert Bly and Harvey Shapiro and my editor.

But that's not all the work I've got. No. So it couldn't be called a "collected." A "collected" would take three or four volumes and, anyway, a "collected" is a dead man's game.

1970

An Interview

With Alan Ziegler

I'd like to start with your evaluation of Pound's legacy.

Pound remains a great poet for me, in bits and pieces, in short poems and in a number of cantos, those in which his lyric impulse is given full freedom. Without question, he was the organizer and leader of the new movement in American poetry. He has set in motion a kind of poetry that remains dominant in America to this day: the poem of direct confrontation with the facts, in language equal to the task, language as direct and hard as the material itself. He has given us other techniques: the power of irony and social commentary, the necessity for strict form as manifesting clear, cogent thought. He was genius for our time. He will always be remembered as Whitman-like at his best, in his desire to open himself to the world and be led too. That these beautiful directions in him may also have led him to insanity—it should be studied. He probably was not temperamentally able to handle it all, but we have his best with us and that will suffice for ages.

You graduated from high school during the Depression and didn't get a college education, is that right?

I did go to Brooklyn College one semester for an evening course and had to quit after that; there wasn't enough money. I didn't learn very much except that the instructress was anti-Semitic. I told her for my end-term paper I was going to do a study of Joseph Conrad and she called me up after class to tell me in a very confidential way that Joseph Conrad was Jewish, to imply that this was not a proper study of English literature. So I acted very innocent about it; I couldn't find the answer to that kind of comment from a teacher. I left and didn't return, and that completed my college education.

How did you make a living?

My work with WPA followed within a year—on the writing project. Then for a while, I was, in effect, a garbage collector. I sat in the office of an incinerator plant and took records of the garbage tonnage that trucks brought in.

You also worked in your father's bindery.

Well, I was in and out of that place, I was having a lot of trouble with the place. At first my father, in all sincerity, offered to pay me a full day's salary for a half day's work, because he was quite concerned about my "obsession," as he called it, with the writing of poetry. We got along very well for a couple of years on that basis. But then he was getting pressure from other directions, and the number of working hours started to increase. At that point I realized I was phasing myself out as a poet, so I just quit and I went looking for four to twelve shifts, like in the sanitation department, the health department, then in hospital work. During the Second World War, I worked in a shipyard as a handyman with a twenty-two pound sledge.

You said once, "I wrote from the position of the worker sensitive to his fate, in the hope that it would penetrate the worker who might already have inured himself to his fate." Were you able to reach your fellow workers through your poetry?

Very few people, if any, knew I was writing those early years. No one really wanted to know what I was doing outside the job itself. I didn't publish my first book until I was thirty-five, and between the ages of eighteen and thirty-five I had published two poems. I was really struggling with myself as a poet, trying to find my style, perhaps hitting it now and then. So, my sense of myself was really very much more absorbed in trying to keep a house together, trying to balance that with writing at night while maintaining my emotional and mental balance at work. It was a real juggling act. Of course, I saw myself identified with the worker in this strain to earn a livelihood for my family. But I was not convinced that this same worker could identify with me as a poet writing about his and my problems—I could sense that from talks with him on and off the job. He could never take seriously what I had to say in my poems, hardly identifying with the bitter spirit, since a worker always remains determined to earn more money—the one criterion and emotional incentive he understands or allows himself to understand and live by. In my poems about working and earning a living for the family, I was questioning the whole point of it in a society that was utterly heartless and cold toward itself in its passion for money and comforts—a paradox, I agree, but as evident today as then. Men and women slave themselves to death for an extra buck.

I rejected it all in practice and in poetry. The only persons reading my poetry at that time and appreciating it were my wife, and Brom Weber, the biographer of Hart

Crane, Milton Hindus during his Céline days, and one or two other friends. No, I wasn't getting my message across to the workers with whom I worked and lived in the same condition and atmosphere. It was an impossibility from the start. Perhaps it was here that my sense of hollowness began and has pursued into the seventies.

There is much suffering in your poetry and your notebooks. Philip Dacey wrote that you are triumphant not over suffering, but in suffering. Do you think it's accurate to say that by confronting suffering head-on and making some sense of it, you somehow transcend the pain?

That's correct. It was some kind of a defensive measure on my part. I thought of it as a means of therapy—coming home, terribly distraught about the day's work—you had to compose yourself, I'm sure I'm not speaking only for myself, it's more than likely that this is the way most art has to be done, under very severe pressures. And the artist who faces these pressures, and brings them out into the open and manages to form a mood of independence, finally, through these sufferings has really triumphed over his material.

In an early poem you wrote, "Get the gasworks in a poem."

That was an aesthetic I had to grasp in its entirety during those years when this was the life that all of us were leading, the 1930s and the early 1940s when we had little to hope for in the way of improvement of our economic and social conditions. We were still in the Depression, we were all in a muddle, we were trying to find our way through. You can look at the paintings of those years, they were struggling with the same material. I was echo-ing, in a way, the mood of the time, and I was groping for the right formula with which to approach it. This was the formula, "get the gasworks," that I discovered for myself. You're of the world and are constantly inter-acting with it, so how can you possibly reject it, without, in a way, rejecting yourself?

Your style is to use the common idiom. It's ironic that your writing may never get into the right eyes. The people who can most empathize may never read it.

That's the irony of it. You'll find poems and entries in the notebooks in which I'm reassessing Whitman's impact upon American thinking and history. It took me some time to realize that he was a deeply isolated writer, who had maybe a handful of friends among Americans. His greatest audience was outside the country. This came in on me gradually as I lived the kind of life that most people were living. There was no choice for me. When Whitman as an inspiration came up in my poetry, I had to deal with it truthfully. I finally realized Whitman was a literary person, not a poet for the working class at all.

Whitman was more optimistic than most poets today.

He had philosophical motivations; he was seeking some-how to ground Eastern philosophy in Western experience. He was trying to bring out that America was the one idealistic nation in the world which all men were looking to with hope. I still think the mainstream in American po-etry is the Whitman tradition. You have Galway Kinnell in the Whitman tradition, Gary Snyder, Allen Ginsberg, George Oppen. The strength of the Whitman tradition remains, but it's there in its negative aspect—America is criticized from the standpoint of having disappointed itself, going to the opposite of what it had intended in the first place.

I think your work complements Ginsberg. The two of you tell what America's about.

Yes. We both write from an uprooted point of view—I speak from the middle and lower middle class, and he from the "unclass." He's searching for affirmation in the spirit, and I'm looking for it around me in nature.

You've written a lot of political poetry, especially about the Vietnam war. How do you relate to your political poetry?

You write to acknowledge your helplessness, you want to reconcile yourself with yourself.

Do you feel that it can go beyond that, that there's any hope of influencing people through poetry?

Well, not immediately, no. Poetry has never played, that I know of, that kind of political or social role in this country. Can I say with any conviction that my poetry has created any difference in the social conditions or in the political conditions; is there any direct relationship? Of course there's no direct relationship but these are hidden matters.

I guess I'm looking for an optimistic answer, although I'm pessimistic myself. A poem should go right down to the root, be radical in the literal sense, and if that can't be a vehicle for getting to people, what is? Political rhetoric is so empty.

It's possible that as the work continues to be read, it'll create a climate of opinion—not only mine, but mine in conjunction with others writing on the same themes: Bly and Snyder, Ginsberg and Oppen. I know for a fact that in the early 1960s, when Bly began to tour the country denouncing the government for its Vietnam policies and writing his antiwar poems, he was instrumental in awakening the campuses to the whole problem. He began making an impact: his readings, his presence, excitement, passion, his hatred of the Vietnam war, not only the poems, but by his fiery defiant statements. Bly was one of the very first. Then the rest of us began to join him.

Perhaps one reason poetry rarely gets to the masses is the way it's often taught in school.

It's been that way for a long time. They don't teach it correctly. They teach it as some sort of mathematical problem: "Look it has meter, it has rhyme, notice how many syllables in the line, notice the different accents—and when you read it, you must read it that way." That's not the way to teach poetry. It should be taught as a communication of recognizable emotions that have been put in their most direct, vivid form in order for the impact to be that much greater than it would be if it were just through ordinary conversation.

What was your impetus to keep the notebooks so assiduously over the years?

I would sit down at night and tell myself the immediate thoughts that were going through my mind, to perhaps gradually evolve from these thoughts an image or a metaphor that would sum up the whole thing. It would often be the beginning of a poem. For the last several years, I've been writing on the typewriter. Until then, I filled notebooks. When *Notebooks: 1934-1971* is published late this year, you'll see about twenty-five poems, each at the end of a particular passage where the poems originated.

How do you feel about your private thoughts being published?

They're not so private. People tell me these are thoughts that they live with every day of their lives.

How do people you are close to feel about winding up in poems about unpleasant experiences or feelings?

All artists have problems with their closest and nearest, nothing ever works smoothly. Who the hell wants anything smooth, anyway? There are moments in your life when you have to be outspoken and direct to unburden yourself. There are other moments absolutely spectacular, you just love yourself and love everyone around you.

When you're writing about a negative experience and it turns out to be a good poem, do you smile?

Oh yeah, sure, I love it. Of course I love it. The main thing is not to use it as a sledge hammer on someone, but to give a rounded picture of what life's all about.

Isn't it also a way of controlling your fate—taking something unpleasant and using it to make something beautiful or meaningful?

Precisely, that's what I was calling therapy—taking a bitter moment, a very difficult moment, and writing about it so that you find yourself in it and independent of it at the same time. By writing about it you affirm the experience, but you affirm the power of creating the experience also. In creating the experience, you've confirmed your power to survive it. You create an act of independence and you are once more free, at least after the poem—for the next half hour or so.

Until the next poem comes. What's your approach to reading your poems in public? You've tried to retrieve the original impulse of the poem at times.

I've tried that. There are times when I might want to study the poem as I remember having written it, and like an actor I will make an effort to have a total recall, but I never really completely succeed. I also have to take into account that I may be in a special mood at that particular time and since I want to be perfectly natural in my delivery, I can't stop to study what the mood was like several years ago. So I often read from the feelings that the poem gives me at the moment.

I've always found your poem "Rescue the Dead" to be enigmatic.

It will always be enigmatic. I look at it several different ways:

Rescue the Dead

Finally, to forgo love is to kiss a leaf,
is to let rain fall nakedly upon your head,
is to respect fire,
is to study man's eyes and his gestures
as he talks,
is to set bread upon the table
and a knife discreetly by,

is to pass through crowds
like a crowd of oneself.
Not to love is to live.

To love is to be led away
into a forest where the secret grave
is dug, singing, praising darkness
under the trees.

To live is to sign your name,
is to ignore the dead,
is to carry a wallet
and shake hands.

To love is to be a fish.
My boat wallows in the sea.
You who are free,
rescue the dead.

Is the last line sarcastic?

That's a piece of irony, because it can't be done. It's a piece of sarcasm to those who think they are free. No one's really free. So, those who think they are, well, the poem says go ahead and show how free you are by rescuing those who are dead, who are not free. When I say, "to forgo love is to kiss a leaf," it's a leap from an abstraction to the concrete instance which disproves the possibility of forgoing love—you can't really forgo love because like a leaf it too is organic, a leaf of the body. It's an affirmative statement put in the negative in preparation for an ironic conclusion.

Your early work tended to be more direct and objectivist than some of your later work.

I've explored many techniques: symbolist, surrealist, the metaphysical approach, hard realism, satire, irony, short lyrics. The mode changes as the mood changes. I've written many poems on the aesthetic of poetry. "Get the Gasworks" was one of the earliest—there are others that are much later, toward the end of the "Collected." For example, "Feeling with My Hands," which starts, "Will this poem be able to think and breathe and have sex?" I moved away from the harsh, direct, objective kind of realism, moved away not because I'm intentionally moving away to show myself in a different frame—it's because the circumstances have changed. My history has changed, the history around me has changed. The literary need to recreate yourself, recreate your whole sensibility, is personal history in action. But the need to act in a particular phase wears out with time and effort. It becomes tiring and you replace it with a new sensibility which begins the whole process over again of excitement and involvement and thinning out. You go on to other ways of sustaining yourself as a poet. Also, there's a certain pride in keeping up with the changes within and without. For example:

The Bagel

I stopped to pick up the bagel
rolling away in the wind,
annoyed with myself
for having dropped it
as it were a portent.
Faster and faster it rolled,
with me running after it
bent low, gritting my teeth,
and I found myself doubled over
and rolling down the street
head over heels, one complete somersault
after another like a bagel
and strangely happy with myself.

I would never have thought of writing that in my twenties and thirties because then I was obsessed with the social condition. But now I realize the social condition is as strongly in me as it is outside of me. So, when I deal with the social condition today, I think of it in terms of myself, knowing what I reflect, how I've been conditioned, that all of history is in me, especially all of the history of the last fifty years. And when I write, I write of *me*.

You left the business world and started teaching in the mid-1960s, did your change of life-style free you to be able to sit down and reflect more than before?

Yes, in the 1950s and early 1960s I worked steadily for my father's bindery, eventually becoming president of the firm. When he died, I liquidated the firm. Once I began teaching, which gave me more leisure, I was able to develop a poem at greater length and go on to assimilate other influences in poetry, like the surrealist mode and others, and create a different body of work, out of a new stance. My surrealist poems are an entirely different mode of writing from the 1930s and 1940s. This is the mode that came up very fast with me in the 1960s. I had to project a distorted view of life that had come over me, that is, I thought the country was in a distorted phase, out of its natural instincts. "Ritual Three" is a poem of brutality, a poem of indifference and cynicism, of man killing man as if it were the necessary right thing to do, as a culture. This is what I saw in the 1960s and I had to write it.

What do you see in the 1970s?

There's a kind of hollowness at the center of things. That has been happening, I suppose, for ever so long, with T. S. Eliot making us conscious of it in *The Waste Land*. There's a hopelessness, or at least a helplessness, among our educated classes. We wonder, what's happened to our ideals, our culture, where we're going. We ask when will we discover ourselves renewed and refreshed and on the way. What we're doing now is playing with different life-styles, with no one way especially significant for us, which is an acknowledgment of emptiness. You take a poem by James Tate, for example. At its most extreme, it's utterly incomprehensible. But it's deliberately incomprehensible because he can't find any meaning to his own life, and he wants to say, "This is how incomprehensible it is to *me*." Then in other poems, he lets you get a peep at what he's thinking and shows himself in a very futile mood and it becomes very clear what he's going through. In style, it comes a little closer to the poem of observed experience. But at his most extreme, he writes with a great density for the purpose of confusing and creating a darkness.

Is there anyone going beyond this, perhaps writing a visionary poetry of what will come out of this darkness?

Hopefully Bly, perhaps Merwin. I know I'm trying, whether in writing or in thinking to myself. I look for a numinous quality.

A lot of your recent poetry is about death; yet, there's a lot of humor in your poetry.

Why not? It's kind of funny having to die, don't you think so? To be serious about life and then suddenly . . . oops, it's all over, and you want to say, "What the hell, what do you mean all over, I haven't finished my sentence." You can't because your mouth is shut.

In your notebooks, you referred to some of this work as rehearsals for your own death. Do you look at this as the same kind of exorcising that you employ when you write about the war, but more personal?

Precisely.

It's been said that death is a more taboo subject than sex in America.

Why it should be so, I don't know. There is no life without death, there is no death without life. Life moves by constant renewal—"death is the mother of beauty," which is Stevens's line, and it's a way of saying that life can only renew itself through death. Something has vanished and life has to assert itself in another form. Something is always becoming still, and yet something is always becoming active.

You spoke about the hollowness of the 1970s. How are you personally reacting to it?

In general, I can do nothing except what comes out in the poetry and that is not always under my control. I can't forsee what I'm going to write. I may have an idea of what I want to say, but the saying of it often turns out to be radically different from what I might have hoped for. If I say now that I want to write a poetry of transcendence—and I've said it to myself many times—I can only be sure that I've talked and thought about it, but not created it in the poem. I do recognize a new voice in my poetry, perhaps a more calm voice of wisdom—what's that?—acceptance of natural processes and events, setting history, the city, culture, work, angers and fears, ambition, love and sex in a natural order that I sense—can it be called transcendence? At any rate, I sense a natural order in things and would like to abide by it. But the poem is paramount; that ultimately determines how convincing I am in this search and so far the answer has yet to come. Perhaps age gives me a sense of perspective which I confuse with a sense of natural order. At any rate, I work with what I have, what I am at the moment and that certainly is a different order of existence than what I learned to understand in the 1930s and 1940s. Many of my poems from nature could give a clue as to where I am at the moment.

There's a lot that goes on in the "literary world" that doesn't have much to do with literature. Do you find a lot of back scratching and biting?

There's a lot of back scratching, that's all I know. How it's all managed I don't know. I'm not in with the back scratchers. Occasionally I hear stories how so and so has arranged for so and so to win the next National Book Award. It's entirely possible, given the atmosphere in which we live today. If such entrepreneurs exist among writers then obviously they must be needed, probably by publishers who must make a *succes d'estime* of their writers to bulk up the firm's own stature. Commercialism is very self-conscious about itself and will employ middlemen in the arts to negotiate awards, publicity, and so forth. But I can't discount the possibility that many in this racket are motivated by sincere regard for their "winning" writers, and so will allow themselves to pull silly stunts like arranging awards in advance of the actual voting. It's pitiful, without a sense of what the real world is all about.

Who are some poets who have not gotten the recognition they deserve?

Reznikoff for one, George Oppen another, Louis Zukofsky.

How do you feel about your success in poetry? One critic called you "one of the best poets of our time."

Nowadays most anyone with a manuscript of poems can get published, so what's this about success? Finally, we're left only with a sense of our own accomplishment, altogether separated from publication. I would like to have done much more. I shall try to do much more. That's all I can say about success. To be called "one of the best poets of our time" is very gratifying, but what are the standards of judgment? I'm not sure myself. I have a gnawing sense that it's all out there yet to be written.

1973

A Dialogue at Compas

Before we arrived, I was thinking of a format for this sort of discussion. It comes to me as rather an unusual procedure, though I have on occasion sat around with poets and writers and spoken about myself, but I'm more inclined to have other people speak about themselves, which gives me something to think about, because I've thought about myself to such a point where I'm perfectly calm from now on as far as my own opinions are concerned. Airing them would be nothing unusual for me, so I'm asking the people, the poets and teachers, to ask me some questions, get me excited, wake me up. I'm sure those who have read my work have a few questions to ask.

I'll ask you one. What are some of the things about contemporary American poetry that upset you?

The terrible prizes being given out.

What do you mean by that?

Compas: Community Programs in the Arts and Sciences, St. Paul, Minnesota. The questions in this interview were asked by various members of the audience.

Well, they are giving prizes to people who are on the periphery of American poetry.

What do you mean, "on the periphery"?

Well, you see I have raised a very important issue in American poetry today. John Ashbery is a very fine poet, but he's not an American poet in the sense that we understand what the mainstream is all about. The mainstream in American poetry—I'll probably get myself all worked up on this subject—the mainstream in American poetry derives from Walt Whitman. It's not so much a celebration of the country or the people in it, but a celebration of oneself, and not oneself as a self, but as a self which is a personification or a surrogate of another power transcending the individual power. And it's not so much a poetry of optimism as a poetry of self-identification with that which exists above and beyond us, whatever it is. Now that, of course, has come into disrepute in the last one hundred years because we question the presence of any unifying sense or principle in the universe. We question ourselves as being surrogates of any kind of divine energy, and American poetry is grappling with this problem, precisely with this very problem; in other words, our best American poets are sons and daughters of Walt Whitman. We are arguing this problem with him. We are asking him, "Are you still viable?" We don't believe he's viable to the extent that he thought of himself as viable. Yet it's a nagging problem, because we can't dismiss this sense of ourselves, as a mystery, a wonder, especially; and it's almost a desolation that we exist without prior knowledge as to our purpose in existing. Whitman thought he had the answers, and Whitman, as the center of our psyche who also brought us a sense of commonality, is not plausible with what we're going through today. But to give him up entirely is to let ourselves sink into something which we just don't want to imagine. So we are at a point now where we talk to him, argue with him, refute him, and when things become very desperate for us, when events in the universe or the world itself bewilder us and throw us into despair, we have an automatic reflex and fall back upon things that he said. We fall back upon the self once more. But that's still not adequate, which is the main problem. We're in a crisis, an intellectual, philosophical, and emotional crisis right now as poets.

John Ashbery is not dealing with this subject at all. Neither is a critic like Harold Bloom. They are critics of *literature*, they are writers of *literature*; they are not writers of life. John Ashbery is fine as a poet of intellectual perception by which he removes himself from the American experience in its actuality, to see himself instead as a reflection of estrangement from ongoing experience. The American poet in the middle stream is totally committed to solving the problem which Whitman handed on to us. But Ashbery is at the periphery of these problems and prefers to see himself separated from them. In other words, when he writes, it's not with a sense of commitment to the problems mentioned before, but rather as involvement with himself in process, simply in process. That is, he avoids discussing what is good and what is wrong, but involves himself in the metaphor of man as simply an ongoing situation or condition. There is no effort to reflect upon the moment or upon an external event. It's simply a constant searching, looking into himself, moving from thought to thought without necessarily evaluating or stopping to evaluate what this thought is and means. It's an evasion and yet it's a form of poetry which has to be respected, precisely because it is genuine with Ashbery.

Now this is a school of poetry that was originally called the New York school of poets. It's an anomaly since most of the poets who came to be representative of that "school" were from out of town: Wisconsin, Minnesota, Oklahoma, Ohio, and so forth. It is very strange because New York poets like myself, like Harvey Shapiro, Armand Schwerner, or Michael Heller, born and raised and educated in New York, are not of the New York school. However it happened, that is beside the point. Originally, this so-called school derived from the influence of certain French poets. Mallarmé would be one. Anyway, there is a French school of poetry, not exactly surrealistic but deriving from surrealism, with no intention of dealing with life as life, but dealing instead with the imagination as an autonomous experience. Of course, that leads poetry into all sorts of strange byways, one of them being Ashbery's concentration on the mind and its values, observations, comments, and associations as merely stuff for processing, to what end we don't know. It is never made clear in the poems, though if we want to listen to the ambiance of sound and to rely too on the movement of the lines, we could say that the meaning is clearly about the irrelevance and the insignificance of anything and everything we experience in ourselves. I hope that I've raised some issues that can be answered or discussed further on in our dialogue here.

I liked the way you said that Whitman thought he had the answer. Do you mean his talking about the purpose of himself and his poems in his poems?

Yes.

And what bothers you is that we don't see that from other people now?

Yes. There's yet another school of poetry, best represented by Kenneth Koch, which thinks of poetry merely as an entertainment—as a higher form of entertainment, without regard to its application to events or individuals who are involved in events. Incidentally, Koch is thought of as a founding member of the New York school. His poetry, I'd say, is a poetry of irrelevance, intentionally so, to distinguish it from Ashbery's, which does not appear to be intentionally irrelevant. With Koch, I feel it's a conscious contrivance as a metaphor for disengagement from social commitment. That's the poetry which, in the last ten years or so, has been gaining prominence at a time when we're probably at the most crucial historical moment in this country: which way are we going to go, as a people. I'm not saying that poetry has to be written as a social commitment—hardly. But poets are living the way all of us live, eating and drinking and making love, and having families and working, so that for most poets the daily life must become the material. Not only the daily life but the life which you carry around within you every day. So it's both the internal and the external that must find themselves on the page. And this is the Whitman tradition. But that isn't the tradition which has gained prominence in the last ten years and been put forward as representative of American poetry at its best.

Is it because Whitman had such a love of life; is it because we don't love life as much as he did?

We are in a dilemma about living; we don't understand what it's all about. We don't understand it.

I'm not sure about understanding it, but how about loving it?

Well, to understand is to love, and since we don't understand what it's about, we're confused, and confusions really don't allow for too much love. When we're desperate, we fall back upon those old assertions that Whitman made, that man is part of the universe and must become identified with the universe. What could be sweeter than thinking of yourself as a tree, as resembling or being identified with a tree, or with the grass or the sun? That's still not enough, you see, it's no longer enough. I can understand why the school of irrelevance exists. And I can sympathize with it because where do we go from our total despair? We go back into ourselves. And when you go into yourself actually you lose touch with yourself. That's the paradox. Once you go too far into yourself you lose touch because your self is only found through interaction with others. I know my poetry is filled with this sort of material, and I've worked through it, but the school of irrelevance wants to say that the self doesn't exist any longer as we used to know it. To look for the self *in* oneself is to lose oneself in oneself. Yet to be related to others is to be related in a contingent manner, in a highly relative manner, in a deeply careful manner—which doesn't fit with the open, embracing forms that we learned from Whitman. We live tentative lives, and the love that you are thinking of, the love for life, is a love which is surrounded and modified, deeply modified, by caution.

Mr. Ignatow, you have a poem about Whitman; it starts something like, "Let us be friends, said Walt." And the poem ends with gravediggers slitting their throats.

The poem is saying negatively everything that Walt put affirmatively. From this, of course, I ask myself, where do I go now? Well, what I do—what I've been doing recently—is falling in love, with anything and everything, and being calm with myself. In fact, I look at the mirror and I enjoy my mustache! Little things like that make a difference, strangely enough. I wish I had the courage to raise a beard; I hope I have one day. I'm awfully glad for this light moment.

There is a poem where you talk about the place in me speaking to the place in you, about centering in your own place so that you can speak to other people's places.

Yes, "My Place." You can see I'm sort of back where I feel I have left long ago. I don't believe in that any longer. I hate to say it, but I really don't believe in it. I feel it's sort of abolished for me. But let me read it.

> I have a place to come to.
> It's my place. I come to it
> morning, noon and night
> and it is there. I expect it
> to be there whether or not
> it expects me—my place
> where I start from and go
> towards so that I know
> where I am going and what
> I am going from, making me
> firm in my direction.
>
> I am good to talk to,
> you feel in my speech
> a location, an expectation
> and all said to me in reply
> is to reinforce this feeling
> because all said is towards
> my place and the speaker
> too grows his
> from which he speaks to mine
> having located himself
> through my place.

In other words, here's an interaction between two persons who find their identity in each other, as two communicants. That's fine for the time being. Just as we're interacting at this moment with each other. But there are so many depths to this thing, this is just the surface. What are we doing except keeping some sort of social contract between us which is very, very frail here. It has no institutional roots. What we're doing is taking something which might have been at one time a religious need, a religious urge, or it might have been a meeting, sort of, where people would confess to one another, very much as at a Quaker meeting—as what we're holding here. But we don't recognize it as such, or we have forgotten that such a thing ever existed. And we don't, we won't buy it. We look upon this meeting between us as really a secular thing. We think that by acting in the secular mode we are not committing ourselves to an outworn, obsolete religion. Nevertheless, this is a religious thing, what we're doing here. We're meeting as a spiritual convention. We're trying to understand each other and trying to affirm each other as persons, to continue to be persons through this meeting, this interaction. We don't wear robes, we're not ministers, but we are carrying on a very sacred act, and the only thing we know that's left to us is to meet this way. Yet it's so tentative, it's so contingent upon shifting circumstance, so that we're here not with the whole mind, not the whole spirit. This is what labors in me all the time. It's a problem which goes beyond my poem of the place. I've yet to formulate that problem or to articulate it as poetry. I'm perfectly willing to—I may have already, it's possible I may have. I think I have, in some poems in *Facing the Tree*. I may have brought this issue out in the open. But this is the issue at the heart of the whole country: are we divided, or are we together? This is where poetry must meet and come forth and record this particular moment. This is not the poetry of irrelevance. This is the poetry of the most painful kind of confrontation. When I see prizes being given for the poetry of irrelevance, I say it is a deliberate act of suicide, in its way. It's a turning of one's back upon what is really rotting America, what is eating at America. It's just deliberate turning away from the disintegrating forces among us, and actually celebrating disintegration.

Do you feel that this manifests itself in other ways, like subject matter or voice in a poem, that is, manifesting itself in diction or use of metaphor, nonuse of metaphor?

If you are referring to techniques and aesthetics, well, of course. A subject of this sort must find its own metaphors and its own materials. That goes without saying. You're talking about form following subject? The organic concept of poetry? That's correct, yes, but even there I've sort of raised questions. I have a number of students at York College and also at Columbia who are writing in stanzaic forms and meter, standard meter and stanzaic forms: the terza rima or the heroic couplet, and iambic pentameter. They insist on working that way, and they're also grappling with issues. Or at least knowing themselves to be disoriented as persons, they get that material into the formal manner of writing—which to me at one point seemed inconceivable. Earlier, say about twenty years ago, it seemed inconceivable that a person who had to confront himself honestly could possibly write in forms imposed upon him. But I've come to realize that there are individuals who can work within imposed forms and write very honestly and well. One such person is Richard Wilbur, who has done what he can to bring these issues into poetry, though he does it with a light touch; and he is very skillful at it and keeps a certain distance from the subject through imposed form. In itself, imposed form is a kind of religion to him.

As it seems to me, by living through form he can maintain himself also psychically; therefore, I am questioning my very roots, my very beginnings, questioning everything that was given to me before I started thinking. When I was in my twenties, I took everything that was given to me without question. I went along by mere instinct. I went directly through instinct. I felt that was where I belonged: I had that—its roots were in my love of the Bible, especially the psalms, which still can move me. They're marvelous to read. And I saw the psalms as the work of artists in organic form, though I learned later that the psalms in their original form were very consciously constructed verse, and that the particular mode in use then, the parallel structures and the repetitions, were what Whitman employed, and so when I fell in love with Whitman's work, it was partly because of my love of the psalms and the Bible as a whole. What goes even beyond that is my impatience at that time with formal poetry. Strangely enough, I was very impatient with it. I can't explain to myself why this was so. It may have been because I suspected the abstract approach to verse which was needed to grasp these forms. By abstract approach I mean the need to analyze the forms for their construction, to take them apart to see what makes them work in meter, rhythm, diction, and so forth, before being ready to invest these forms with your own personality. That impatience is very American, to go headlong into experience without waiting to think first what is happening. So I am an American, God help me, and shall I say that those who are writing in traditional forms are not American? Is that what I'm supposed to say? No, it's not true. It's not true.

But, Mr. Ignatow, how can we be concerned with writing an American poem, which I think we should be con-

*cerned with as American poets, and worry about English
versification and English metrics and stanza forms?*

Well, you must know that the English have a tradition
of the free form just as powerful in its way as ours,
Christopher Smart, for example. Except that the English
establishment has, more or less, ignored it and in some
cases turned its back on it. And significantly, those in
the English tradition of organic form today come from
a class in society that the English were not about to ac-
cept, and still have difficulty in accepting. When you
think of Roy Fisher, a contemporary English poet who
writes in the forms we use in this country—he is virtually
in oblivion, as far as the English establishment is con-
cerned. Yet he and others are remarkably good poets.
But who is a poet respected by the establishment?
Larkin. He writes in traditional English forms. Auden.
Now Auden, when he arrived in this country—that's the
one for whom we should have some animosity—when he
arrived, he introduced the entire English liturgy of tradi-
tional forms once more into the American mainstream
of poetry. Just as Eliot, in his time, brought that same
tradition into American poetry, at the moment that
William Carlos Williams and Ezra Pound were weaning
American poets away from it. Ezra Pound and—no, Eliot
especially, came on the scene to reverse the entire trend
represented by Williams. It was not so much the tradi-
tional forms as such—Eliot himself had on more than
one occasion departed from them—but in his respect
and, I should say, reverence for them, not to speak of
the sensibility that he brought with him that contra-
vened everything of the spirit for which Williams stood;
but eventually, of course, Williams overcame it. The in-
fluence of Williams in conjunction with that of Charles
Olson overcame this English trend in spirit and form in

American poetry, and Williams's work and influence became once more ascendant. Auden had gradually infiltrated the American literary world, and Auden is, I'd say, the progenitor in some respects—which it would be difficult for me at this time to delineate—of the school of irrelevance. Because he's a detached poet in his last work, and, if you don't know this it will come to you as a shock, he rejected all his own early work. He virtually refused to have anything to do with it; he refused to recognize it as work deriving from his innermost being. He preferred the poems of the last twenty years of his life, didactic, discursive, and virtually expository. Also steeped in religion in a sense which goes even further than Eliot's, in certain ways. Anyway, it's there. We have it, and we simply can't ignore it. And it's being absorbed. So I would say that this is still the minor tradition in this country. Our major tradition remains the Whitman tradition.

I'd like to ask you a question. It's something that I've tried to answer, never very successfully. If we don't have verse forms to work in, if we don't have these impositions of the past to put on the poem, what is it that we have right now that distinguishes itself as poetry? What goes on in our writing that we can call a poem, if we're not concerned with versification?

Well, how many of you know the work of Christopher Smart? Do you know the history of the reception of his work, in his time?

Very poor.

Very poor. It was virtually ignored. You know, Blake has become important and influential only since the early twentieth century, but in the eighteenth and nineteenth centuries he was dismissed. Now what today makes us feel and think of Smart as a great poet? "Jubilate Agno." What makes us think of it as a great poem? It's the vision. What makes Blake a great poet? It's the overpowering concept or insight that he has, around which everything forms, toward which everything is drawn. And it's the work of prose. I am referring to his visionary poems. Let's call it prose poetry. Prose poetry begins in France; I mean as an actual form, an actual formal approach to poetry. It's only recently that we've begun to accept prose poetry as a new mode for us, a formal mode of poetry. I've been writing many prose poems. Michael Benedikt is editing an international anthology of prose poets, and it should be out by the end of this year—which will finally nail down, once and for all, that poetry doesn't necessarily have to have traditional stanzaic patterns. It's vision that counts. Anything that's held together by an insight, around which everything gathers and goes towards and helps build—that is a poem. You can take pages out of Joseph Conrad, long, long pages out of his novels, which are remarkably good prose poems. There are others, Faulkner, for example. You can read him and think that you're in the midst of a fantastically beautiful prose poem about the woods and the land. He's marvelous about the woods and the land. So the English formal tradition is narrow, and yet it has great poets, no question about it.

Robert Bly in the Selected Poems *finds in your work a touch of the compression that Hemingway has in his short stories. Do you agree with that?*

Oh, I would think so, yes. When the University of New Mexico had a magazine of some prestige years ago— Edwin Honig at the time was at the helm of it—they were publishing signatures of poets. At that time they published a signature of eight poems of mine and asked me for a statement, and in that statement I singled out Hemingway as one of my masters for his colloquial style and for its bareness, virtually stripped language which I thought had to be—but it was so typically in the voice of American speech. So I always strove for simplicity and directness in my poems. In fact, one of his rules was to avoid adjectives like the plague. I went through my work meticulously, scrupulously eliminating adjectives where I could. As a result, the emphasis was put on the verb. That is, the responsibility of the poem, the movement of the poem was put upon the verb. Now the verb, as a result, would either show up, after eliminating the adjective, to be strong enough to stand on its own or had to be revised upward, more intensely. That, of course, led to a dramatic way of writing, you see. In other words, what Hemingway was about, really, was to dramatize experience and not to be simply descriptive. Adjectives tend to color a thing, whereas a verb, emphasis upon a verb, tends to give the poem a whole new power. In brief, it gives it a kind of explosive force. You're really getting at the heart of the subject for me when you talk about the aesthetics of Hemingway. I think he is one of the great stylists we have—and he's a poet. In many of his short stories there is a sense of prose poetry. You probably know that he wrote a good many poems, which don't compare to anything he's written in prose. In his poems he had a false conception of what poetry was. If you had told him that he was writing prose poetry in his best work, he'd probably have been very scornful of the idea. Well, that reminds me of an anecdote about myself. I was writing, years ago, with the intention of making a million dollars as a *Saturday Evening Post* writer. I began to write long stories. That's what they wanted, long stories, about a couple meeting on a liner, a Cunard liner, on the way to England, and falling in love and going through all the tribulations of two persons already married. That sort of thing. Well, I submitted that story, and I went to great lengths to describe the emotional tensions between the two, and within themselves, and I tried to be as vivid as possible. It was sent back with a note: "This is a very poetic prose. I don't think we can use it." And it kind of shook me. "I don't want to write poetry, I want to make money," I told myself in bafflement. That was my feeling then. Those were the years, in the 1930s, when there was really rough going, and I thought I was going to help my family by becoming a writer, immediately winning $5,000 for a story that I could knock off in a short time. I kept writing, despite the rejection. I was very stubborn, and I'd submit my stories to other magazines, and they'd keep telling me I was writing poetic prose, not a story. "We don't want poetic prose. We want a story, with a beginning, a middle, and an end, and stick to the facts." Well, I decided on writing poetry, giving up my dream of enriching my family, and I sent one or several poems—can't remember now—to Theodore Weiss, editor of the distinguished *Quarterly Review of Literature,* which was one of the very first to support William Carlos Williams, Ezra Pound, and e. e. cummings in their then innovative styles, and the poems came back with cryptic comments about their lack of this and that. I tried several more times and got the same response. Bitterly, I sent off a letter, a long letter of complaint to him and about him. Here I had turned to poetry, after having been rejected as a prose writer, and now I was being rejected by the editor of a magazine who surely knew what poetry was. And back came his reply full of praise and admiration for my letter of prose. It was, to him, the best thing yet I had sent to him. It was my prose poetry again being praised.

Mr. Ignatow, I write fiction myself, and people say, "Oh, this is poetic, this is poetic fiction. Why don't you write fiction fiction*?"*

You're in trouble.

I'm wondering if there's a connection between that impulse, to say this is poetic fiction, not fiction fiction, the popularity, or whatever, of the poetry of irrelevance.

I don't know. All I know is that there are writers, novelists, today who are writing poetic prose, like Bartheleme, for one, and sometimes Vonnegut, and what they've done is to take over the techniques, perhaps the total mode of poetic prose, of poetry itself. They write metaphors, really. Bartheleme takes a metaphor and pursues it right through to make of it a story, and that's what prose poetry is doing too. Actually, he writes prose poems, long prose poems, sometimes disconnected on purpose.

Is that what you're doing in your poem "A Political Cartoon"?

Yes, yes. Well, I wrote that as a happening. Do you recall in the 1960s when happenings were popular? They were spontaneous, original, to begin with, and then they were arranged and thought out in advance. Well, I wrote this as a happening, and it was performed in New York.

With a truck? With a truck coming in?

Not exactly. It was performed in East Hampton. He came in with a horse and wagon. It was very funny. We did it out in the open fields.

Getting back to what we were talking about as far as compression goes, use of verbs. Can you talk a little about how Gertrude Stein uses verbs, and how you feel about her work?

Well, *The Making of Americans,* to me, begins marvelously well, and then it runs downhill. I can't continue to read it, somehow. You're right about the use of verbs there. The emphasis is on verbs, constant movement. I think it's for that reason, the repetition of one verb, that it gets on my nerves after a while.

I want to ask the names of some of the women poets you recognize as good.

Diane Wakoski.

Women who use powerful verbs.

Who use verbs primarily? Well, there, Diane Wakoski.

Those closest to what you imagine is the ideal.

Denise Levertov, Marge Piercy, Adrienne Rich, although Rich tends to intellectualize her work, her vision. Diane Wakoski deals with events always, and her work may be prosy but at its best it's very powerful because she moves you with events, and events, of course, that are moved by verbs. She's not sparing of action. Action, for her, is the metaphor of her existence. In other words, she's not an intellectual poet, as is Rich. In Rich there's a constant presence of theory working its way through to a conclusion, whereas with Wakoski there's always a sense of an experience being resolved. That's the difference between them. Although they're both good poets—each in her own way—I would prefer Wakoski. Marge Piercy I would relate to Wakoski. There are other poets; there are some marvelous black women poets around—Lucille Clifton, she's just beautiful. When she uses verbs out of a dialect—she could speak the language of a professor any day of the week—she uses the black dialect naturally. The verbs there—now black dialect is precisely the language of verbs. That's what's so interesting about it. Where I teach, at York College, I'm simply bowled over by the vividness with which they write when they write informally. There's another very fine black poet out in Oregon. I visited him there recently. Primus St. John. Anyone heard of him?

He's been here.

Marvelous man. He's a great poet. Did he read from his book, *Skins of the Earth*? Well, he must have, he probably did. He's another man who's on his way to a Ph.D., but he will not, he has not cut himself off from his roots. When he writes, he writes with the power of his remembrance. He may be at a distance from the actual place where he was raised, but he does not intend to give it up because that is the blood and tissue of his work. Now that is what great poetry is about. That is what I would hold as distinct from the poetry of irrelevance. That's the difference. The poetry of irrelevance is primarily intellectual. It's the search for autonomy through the intellect, primarily, as the embodiment of all there is to feel and know. It's once more a man falling back upon his mind as the last recourse in life. He no longer has faith in his body. In the work, say, of Kenneth Koch or John Ashbery, they don't think body experiences amount to very much because of their transient, ephemeral character which, to Koch and Ashbery, are too weak for that reason to give value to life. Which is just the opposite of the work and purpose of Primus St. John. Just the opposite of the work of Walt Whitman. If any people are carrying on the tradition of Walt Whitman in his forms and attitudes, it would be the Puerto Ricans and the blacks, because they are upward moving people. They are forcing their way through the hard crust of American life, asserting themselves in the only way they know how, and that is through the tradition that they must grasp, the tool they must grasp to survive and prosper, the Walt Whitman thing.

Is there some relation between that and the upsurge of the women's movement?

Absolutely.

What kind of energy do you find distinctive about the poetry of the women's movement?

The energy of opening oneself, of opening up one's experiences to the world. It's primarily based upon and rooted in experience. Coming out of experience and speaking about experience. Projecting experience, honest experience. Totally. Again, that's the tradition of the midstream of American poetry; that's just what doesn't get its proper applause and recognition. It may with time, I think, and the fact that, if you don't mind my saying it, with the *New York Times* at the center, one of the central influences in contemporary literature, and Harvey Shapiro as book editor there—himself one of our finest poets—we can have high hopes.

I want to get back to your comments about compression and Hemingway's realism.

I hope I can too.

I read through your books in these last couple of weeks, and I get a feeling you're doing something almost like Kafka, now and then. Strange things start to happen. I know there's a poem in there called "News Report."

Well, that's an early one.

Very Kafkaesque.

That's an early poem. Kafka was important, always has been important to me. In fact, I recently wrote some Kafkaesque poems, but that is something arbitrary on my part. I feel disoriented like Kafka; I feel imprisoned in myself like Kafka; and when I say all this, I say it not as a unique thing, it's not something unique to me; it's something I feel each of us is experiencing. So Kafka has relevance to the contemporary scene as far as I'm concerned. That's a technique also—a technique I took over, which I decided to use after I became kind of satiated with the use of poetry of direct observation, externally and internally. I decided I ought to give myself an exercise in imaginative constructions that aren't necessarily related to direct experience or observed experience. So it led me to enter into Kafka's territory, but it wasn't done consciously. In other words, when I decided that I was going to write "imaginatively," I would begin with something very improbable, an improbable statement, and seek to make it plausible for myself by using materials that would generally apply to direct observation. I would use incidents and develop that improbable statement, using such incidents in relation to it, as Kafka does—incidents you would generally associate with everyday existence. In other words, I'd lull you into believing that this improbable event could actually happen. Well, Kafka did that with "The Hunger Artist," if you recall, and also with "The Metamorphosis." That's his technique over and over again, but I only realized it when I began reading him.

Are people uncomfortable with that? When I read "The Bagel" I really liked it, but—

Well, you don't have to be ashamed of that.

I was, in a way.

You were? I suspected it.

I felt like I wasn't supposed to like it because it wasn't direct observation.

Well, this sort of poem introduces a whole new element into American poetry. There is a European influence, if I may put it that way. Yet, let's look back on Poe. Poe's work is generally surrealistic in tone, his short stories, and it's not a new stream.

"Bartleby the Scrivener"?

Bartleby is the personification of a surrealist character, yes, of a kind. We've had it all the while in American literature, that thread of surrealism running through. But we only became aware of it as material for poetry when translations flowed into this country from different places. We recognize it now as a mode that we've always had which yet is something new for us to develop, that is, to go back to old sources and reestablish ourselves in them. I feel it's not irrelevant to the American mainstream to use the mode of surrealist poetry. But we're not really writing surrealist poetry; what we're doing is taking its techniques and giving them a form and a meaning which surrealist poetry rejects. Honest-to-goodness surrealist poetry will have nothing to do with meanings clearly stated and accessible. But we don't use surrealism in that sense: we use the improbable, we use fantasy more than anything else. When I said "Bartleby" was surrealistic, I overstated the case; it's really a fable—it's the use of the fable.

Like Kafka's?

Yes, that's right. These are fables, fable methods, not really surrealism.

There's a relation I see between going away from the world into something like the poetry of irrelevance and going away from the world into a fable. I think my uncomfortableness is some confusion of these two. I have the feeling that if I'm going away from the world into fable, maybe I'm going into irrelevance too.

I'm awfully glad you brought me back to this because I had in mind discussing the use of direct observation in poetry. What remains probably still the most powerful mode that we have in American poetry is experience written about directly—some of Richard Hugo's best work, for example. That is the kind of writing which Whitman gave us. We have only to look through "Song of Myself" to see how some of the incidents which he describes that were so shocking to the nineteenth century are today quite mild. But there it is; there's the tradition begun by Walt Whitman, direct observation in the context of a sort of transcendental evaluation of these observed experiences. What we've done is to eliminate the transcendental evaluation and, extracting the whole technique of direct observation, made it the force, the main force, rather than the transcendentalism. We've made realism the power. To find yourself attracted to the fable is not a departure from realism in any sense; it's a deepening in some ways. What a fable does is get at the essence of the experience in its, shall I say, spiritual sense? In other words, the fable will be a metaphor for one's insight into reality. It's a kind of shorthand to writing a very lengthy novel. That's the way I found it. I was writing poetry when I was desperately yearning to be a dramatist also. I tried drama too; I wrote four plays. This was at a time when drama had no possibility at all; there was just no money around for it. We had only the Group Theater at that time. The Group Theater in those years had its select playwrights, such as Odets, Lawson, and one or two others; that was the entire theater community then. There was the Theater Guild, but that was all Eugene O'Neill, and they wouldn't go beyond that—Eugene O'Neill and Behrman. So when I put my plays aside, I was still preoccupied with the dramatic means of writing. I had so many plays and short stories with no hope for them; I put them in my drawer and decided to do the shorthand thing, and that is when I finally committed myself to writing poetry, when I decided that I was going to do these short stories and dramas as poems. The poem is the shorthand form for me—to write a very strong summary or brief or digest of a long short story. There are many poems in my books which began years before as short stories that I simply summed up in ten lines of poetry, ten concrete lines. Now the fable is precisely in the same direction. There is much to say, yet a metaphor has the virtue of putting together ten different strands, constructed properly, in a fable. How about my reading a couple of poems and then talking about them, some recent work? This will be a poem that I can call an invented dream. Not a dream that you have at night, but a dream which uses the improbable made to sound plausible.

> I sink back upon the ground, expecting to die. A voice speaks out of my ear, You are not going to die, you are being changed into a zebra. You will have black and white stripes up and down your back and you will love people as you do not now. That is why you will be changed into a zebra that people will tame and exhibit in a zoo. You will be a favorite among children and you will love the children in return whom you do not love now. Zoo keepers will make a pet of you because of your round, sad eyes and musical bray, and you will love your keeper as you do not now. All is well, then, I tell myself silently, listening to the voice in my ear speak to me of my future. And what will happen to you, voice in my ear, I ask silently, and the answer comes at once: I will be your gentle, musical bray that will help you as a zebra all your days. I will mediate between the world and you, and I will learn to love you as a zebra whom I did not love as a human being.*

Do you want to make any comments on the poem? I'm perfectly willing to listen.

---

*This poem is now printed as a prose poem, its original form, in *Tread the Dark*.

Well, one thing I think of is that stripes suggest one of the earliest ways to organize existence—organize reality— is putting stripes on something.

Putting stripes on someone. That's an interesting view I hadn't really considered. Can you enlarge upon it?

I don't know much more; I came across it in something I was reading. It's a book called Number and Time *by Marie Von Franz. She mentions it.*

That's interesting—to think that I'm organizing time and space and life according to stripes—black and white stripes—that's very interesting.

In that poem you've touched on a whole field we haven't talked about: those poets who imagine themselves like shamans, transformed into animals, poets such as James Dickey, Ted Hughes, and John Haines. Do you know this group of poets?

Yes, but I treat this theme from an ethical point of view.

Is that because you're in the zoo?

That's because I'm a Whitmanite, stuck with the ethical point of view. Whitman, if anything, was a poet of ethics, a poet of conduct, of behavior, of manner, though he wanted, intended to override it all by another vision, a superior vision. Do any of you know his "Democratic Vistas," by the way? That's a very powerful indictment of a whole new social system that arose after the Civil War. He says explicitly what's wrong. It still applies to our present situation. Yet he recovers to speak about the future. You know what is so characteristic about American life and living: we're always living for the God-damned future. If you live for now, you just fall to pieces, because what is *now*? *Now* is a process, a movement. That word "process" relates back to Ashbery. A process, we know, is a lack of or loss of identity; it becomes an anonymous thing.

Early in the zebra poem you mention that "a voice speaks out of my ear." I was wondering if this was an intentional effort to reverse the process of hearing coming into the ear—in other words, the voice speaks from inside my ear.

Some people might say it's the voice of the soul or the voice of one's conscience. Notice how this poem is basically a poem of conscience—not consciousness but conscience. It's rooted in change, conscience rooted in change.

The change that you seek in the poem is going from unloved to loved?

That's right. A change of oneself. Can one change oneself in one's present human form? What happens in that sort of form; what can we do in that form? All we can do is imagine a change, and this is a projection of an imagined change. It's open to all sorts of discussion, this kind of poem. I read it to invite that. Now this next poem has a technique which maybe I've seen elsewhere, I don't know, but it's based upon the idea that there is such a thing as being autonomous. That is, poetry can write itself. It's a throwback to Dadaism or automatic writing, but it's also a restatement on a different level of automatic writing. Of course, to read it to you is the only way to explain it—which I'll do. Some of my influences do come from Europe, no question about it, but then America was first discovered in Europe, wasn't it, and derived its identity from Europe? We're all immigrants here. So this is a poem which you might say is European, in a way.

I'm a Depressed Poem

You are reading me now and thanks. I know I feel a bit better and if you will stay with me a little longer, perhaps take me home with you and introduce me to your friends, I could be delighted and change my tone. I lie in a desk drawer, hardly ever getting out to see the light and be held. It makes me feel so futile for having given birth to myself in anticipation. I miss a social life. I know I made myself for that. It was the start of me.

I'm grateful that you let me talk as much as this. You probably understand, from experience; gone through something like it yourself which may be why you hold me this long. I've made you thoughtful and sad and now there are two of us. I think it's fun.*

That ending line really rips people apart somehow. It's very perverse, but intentionally so because it's to make you feel more strongly than ever that this poem really made itself. Of course, that's a falsehood—it's really a dramatic device. I've personified the poem as a human being, but what lies beneath is the idea that all poetry is human in essence. This is taking it a step further, to ask why, then, can't a poem be a human being? If all poetry is human in essence, why can't one poem suddenly become human in itself, if it's the seed of humanity?

---

*This poem is now printed as a prose poem, its original form, in *Tread the Dark*.

I get an uneasy feeling when I read poems which talk about poems. I noticed in just a quick reading of Facing the Tree *that there seemed to be a lot of that going on.*

Well, let's see what you mean. Is there any one poem that you are referring to? There's a conscious attention to form and substance. It's not random poetry, if that's what you're referring to.

No, I'm not thinking of random, but the Whitman poem "Poets to Come" comes to mind because of this notion of talking about writing poetry while you're writing poetry. It seems to be a strain that runs through a lot of people's work.

Absolutely—it's characteristic. You've hit upon a very important theme in contemporary poetry. The subject is the poem itself. Of course, we could trace it back to Wallace Stevens. Now what this subject is really saying is that there's a crisis at the heart of creativity. What is a poem? But deeper than that, what is a human being that makes him think he's writing poetry? How does he judge that he's making a form? Where does he get the values? What are his values and where does he get them? How does he know he has values? All this is what the poem is about. A poem is really a concept. Writing about poetry actually is a questioning of the human spirit. And the poem changes from time to time. I've written so many poems about poetry to affirm myself as a poet in one way or another. There were times when I wrote poems which embraced the world around me, poems that are based upon facts. The poem couldn't possibly exist if I hadn't laid out one fact after another. There's one poem I could read you which deals with that. And when I lost faith in facts and my observed reality, when I felt that it was something which was constantly shimmering into different forms, I felt that I just couldn't stay with that kind of writing, the objectivist form of writing. It became for me untenable. I could no longer really hold on to it and have enough faith in it to say that anything I perceived could be perceived in its objectivist form. So I turned back into myself, and I wrote a poem about matters going on inside myself. There I finally recognized that that too was subject to change, extraordinary changes going on right in front of me, the very thing I was talking about was losing its identity. I was writing and becoming something else in the process. So I lost faith in that way of writing, and then I began to see whether I could merge the internal with the external, that is, to write from within out. In other words, allowing for shifting moods and changes of events—events changing too, right before me—and this is at the root of the dilemma about the nature of poetry. It is involved with the evanescence of the human spirit, and revelation is at the root of poetry itself.

Could you talk again about process in John Ashbery. I didn't understand.

Yes. Evidently what I've been saying isn't coming across. It's just a little too vague, is that right?

Well, I didn't understand what process meant in Ashbery.

Okay. Too bad I don't have his work in front of me. When Ashbery records the ideas and feelings going through his mind, he's not letting us understand what lies beneath their surface, why these ideas and feelings happen to emerge at that time. He puts them purely in the forms that they present to him, and when he thinks that there is nothing further forthcoming, that is, when he loses interest in recording them, he just drops it all. Then he'll go on, perhaps the next day, and say, "Well, maybe I'll go back again and start recording. From what I can make of his poems, they are just one lengthy report following another. And by that is meant the process. He's letting you watch him record his thinking and emotional states as they go through.

How would that relate to you and trying to write what you were just talking about, from the internal to the external? Is there any sort of connection?

I must reject his kind of writing because I'm always searching for meaning. I'm always searching for the ultimate sense of what is happening, as if it were possible to find meaning. I don't want to live without meaning. But I am living without meaning, which is the meaning of living without meaning. It's a struggle, in other words. What I do is confront meaninglessness as such, and I state it, whereas Ashbery, rather than being explicit about the meaninglessness of life, uses it merely as a metaphor, by just showing himself going through the process of meaninglessness. I take the events of my life, the actual events of my life, and dramatize them as to their meaning or lack of meaning for myself. That's the difference between us. I do it episodically, where he does it through an internal recording. I do it either through events or a combination of inner and outer, searching for something that signifies or is without signification.

You've talked about objectivism in your early poetry.

One of the things that I like very much about your work is that even though you may be grounded in a lot of reality, there is still a sense of mystery, which for me is very necessary in great poetry. This is where I feel Rakosi and many of the other objectivists fall short. They would not allow fantasy or mystery or celebration into their work.

I've always felt that objective reality was a mirage of some sort.

That's a bitter pill.

I've always felt it was a mirage. I can't to this day pin down motives, for example, for my marriage. I can't to this day pin down the motives for having a child. I can't pin these things down. This is what you go through in life, you circle around the subject again and again. Sometimes you find significance, meaning, sometimes you don't. Generally the very fact that you're constantly circling around it is disastrous for meaning. There is no ultimate meaning, finally. Ashbery is also at work here, but rather than dealing with the subject of meaninglessness, he deals with the whole process of meaninglessness. And that's the difference: it leads to a kind of gentility, a low-keyed detachment from life. Because I still think life has to be lived, no matter how meaningless it is, how difficult it is to grasp the essence, if it has any essence at all. Life still has to be affirmed and expressed in all its ways.

Do you believe the responsibility of the poet is anything more, needs to be more, than the confrontation with entrapment and despair, internal and external? Does it need to be more than the confrontation that you mentioned, with yourself and the world around you? Does it need to propose a future, to propose a change?

I can't propose any change. All I can do is protest what's happening.

Well, you propose a change in the zebra poem.

But that's purely imagined—it's tongue in cheek, purely tongue in cheek. That's about it. I wish I knew what a change was.

At the same time, I think the word "responsibility" seems to be a really important one. I mean if we're thinking about what an artist has to offer to the community of people. The word "responsibility" is that relation. I think it was Ortega y Gasset talking about the devaluation of the role of the modern artist in society: in the middle of the nineteenth century visions which artists steeled themselves for, he said, would make critics today tremble—that they'd try to reach that far. I think it's possible that artists can set examples.

We've lost; that's really what it is. Most poets feel that they've lost that shaman role, the role of the prophet and the magician. It's lost because they're leading ordinary lives; they are not being treated in any special way.

But don't shamans reject outward life, and if that's true, aren't they moving into themselves. I have the feeling that if you're a shaman you move away.

You don't move away from life, no. You know life and

you can manipulate it: a shaman manipulates life. He uses his magic and his extramental powers to arrange life in different ways for people and for himself. That would be the power of the poet too, through the image, through the force of the image, to change the direction of life, or someone's life, even if only his own. This is the power we feel we've lost in our society.

Do you see this as a cultural phenomenon? Is it going on in other places in the world?

Sure.

Is there any substitute, then, for the shaman, or is the shaman voice dead?

No. I think eventually it will have to be recovered by the poet. In fact, the poet who has given up on the shaman idea is lost as a poet.

I agree with that, but I want to say something contrary to what you're saying. To quote Carl Rakosi, who did a workshop right before you—he said that Blake and Robert Duncan were the only poets of shamanistic quality, and the rest of us who try it are simply high-flown and preposterous—which is perhaps the very core of Rakosi's weakness as a poet. He needs a little bit of medicine man in him.

I don't think he felt that those were the only two poets who were shaman types, and that everyone else was preposterous. Maybe you could talk about it.

Well, I think Rakosi has a lovely sense of play and wit.

Once in a while he makes a stab in the dark. Occasionally he'll do that. But he prefers really to dance upon the graves, and it's always entertaining, always charming to hear. It has a kind of Mozartian quality; it's light but it's penetrating.

I wonder if Bly strikes you as being shamanistic?

Bly has a shamanistic quality about his work. Of course, he often fails too. Shamans aren't always on the beam. They can miss their calling; sometimes they don't hear the voice. It's when they hear the voice that they suddenly astound you. Bly's "The Teeth Mother Naked at Last"—I think that is the greatest antiwar poem we've had. It's enormous; it's got power, power beyond power. It just makes you shudder as you're reading it.

I disagree that you can't propose changes, you can only elucidate them. Is that correct?

Yes. You can't propose changes, but you can protest what is.

I think to develop a vision, you've got to propose changes. I mean I think you've got to replace what you're protesting against with something else. I think that's what made the great visionaries.

Well, you can't be specific. The only change that we can really imagine is to affirm ourselves in the positive rather than the negative sense. Do any of you know my "Three Ritual Poems"? Each of them states a human condition, but by the very fact that I state these three terrifying human conditions, I tell you what we must move away from. But you can't lay down what we're moving into, you can't say that. It's not possible when changes are so unpredictable. We can only be general about it.

Don't you think Blake did?

Well, Blake is not of this century. What he says has been said over and over again, and you can't go beyond it.

I think you can. I mean, I think you can take the specifics of this century and go beyond them. I think that's a responsibility that poets today have neglected.

I think the responsibility of the poet today is to take what is—and what should be is problematical.

I disagree.

I don't mind your disagreeing at all. In fact, I hope your poetry eventually gives us a vision of what's to be. That's what we need. That's why I say I've fallen in love with everything. I think that might be the vision I'm asking for, to love. I can't think of anything else to take its place that would recover the loss I feel in human relationships or in the world itself. Just to reassert in some form, any form at all, that we can have or find is affirmation of love, in ourselves and with others. If you want to call that a vision, that's fine. I know what my daughter is going through. She's going on twenty, and she won't have anything to do with the system as it is. She's going into things that are totally outside of the system but need support from the system: she needs support from me to do what she wants to do. So it's a terrible paradox, and I am very much aware of it. I'm in great sympathy with her—what she wants to do—and I will support her to the hilt. But if she thinks it is going to come into reality, here and now—I think she has more sense than that. Still, she has the right to pursue it, up to a point where she begins to recognize what its limitations are. Nevertheless, she has a vision, and I want her to live it to the full. But it has to come through me.

Well, any change needs support of its past because that's how it will be born.

Precisely. But how many of us are tolerant of change to that extent? When we try to change this society into an integrated society, how much change, how much of that vision is being realized today?

Then we go back to the poet.

That's where the poet comes in and rages against segregation. By that meaning he stands for integration. When Bly rages against the Vietnam war, it's because he has a vision of what should be instead. The fact that a man writes bitterly, tragically, is because he or she has a vision which is being destroyed or set aside.

I guess that's what I want to hear more of, then. I want to hear more of the positive vision than the protest.

Funny, but I did choose a lot of positive poems to read tonight. I've been feeling that way lately, wanting to read all those poems of affirmation which have between the lines the struggle to make it real.

I would like to get you talking about Whitman again. I'm puzzled—you say that you're confronting the meaninglessness of life; how are we to take Whitman then? Statements like, America need never be bankrupt while apples grow in the orchards or fish swim in rivers—that doesn't seem enough for us anymore. So how can Whitman still be what we need, or how can he still have this meaning?

I can't support Whitman any longer in his transcendentalism. I take from him certain techniques, and at the last minute we do fall back upon his love of life, his total celebration of life, undefined, unqualified. He gives life his unqualified love. He can love a diseased mind as easily as he can love anything else. He loves all of life. But that is the last resort, when that which we had hoped would come to reality doesn't come, then we fall back once more upon, "Well, we're alive, at least," that sort of thing. That's all I can derive from Whitman; his ideals no longer have any meaning in this country. They couldn't possibly be brought about—talking of brotherhood and comradeship—where? how? It still remains the ideal, in its most diluted form, made statistical and bureaucratic.

I can't imagine, really, that life for Whitman was any cleaner than life for us, you know? I mean, we still have a boundary waters canoe area to escape to, but that's beside the point. When Whitman was living we had the Civil War, we had Boss Tweed, we had immigrants steaming in from abroad, we had black slavery, and we were still wiping out the Indians. Now, to my mind, we're still playing the same game, and that's what it is, a barbaric world.

But Whitman's approach to it, his solution doesn't hold for us any longer. His idea was that we could all transcend ourselves, but his solution—for each of us to transcend our personal selves, our greeds, our lusts, our prejudices, our intellectual limitations, for each of us to transcend and become a whole—doesn't really hold, and didn't even in his time, as he himself recognized during the Civil War. Finally he said that perhaps all his poetry was merely an experiment. He made that statement. So he was the first to reject his own work, to reject the basis of his work.

I think we've been nagging at you ever since you read the zebra poem. This is sort of tongue in the cheek thing—but the zebra, in order to become good, has to be imprisoned.

Has to be imprisoned? Has to be in a zoo.

In a zoo, yes, which is a denial of his nature. It's as though there's this restraint that is necessary in order to be loved.

Love is itself an imprisonment, a form of imprisonment.

Then what we sacrifice, if it is a sacrifice, is ourselves.

Precisely. What I say in "Rescue the Dead"—"To live . . . is to carry a wallet"; to love is to be dragged into the forest in the dark. Would you like me to read that poem? Believe me, I'm not cynical, I'm not skeptical; I'm just grieving. I've never grown up, period. I always want things to be as I thought of them when I was an adolescent. They say that's the problem with American writers, that we're all adolescents.

Rescue the Dead

Finally, to forgo love is to kiss a leaf,
is to let rain fall nakedly upon your head,
is to respect fire,
is to study man's eyes and his gestures
as he talks,

is to set bread upon the table
and a knife discreetly by,
is to pass through crowds
like a crowd of oneself.
Not to love is to live.

To love is to be led away
into a forest where the secret grave
is dug, singing, praising darkness
under the trees.

To live is to sign your name,
is to ignore the dead,
is to carry a wallet
and shake hands.

To love is to be a fish.
My boat wallows in the sea.
You who are free,
rescue the dead.

Well. How about reading a couple more? Let me read
that one poem I talked about in the objectivist mode,
which was a definition of poetry at that time, as I saw
it. In other words, my definitions have been changing
with time, and here's an early definition. It's called "Get
the Gasworks." It's obviously a statement of objectivist
poetry.

Get the Gasworks

Get the gasworks in a poem
and you've got the smoke and smokestacks,
the mottled red and yellow tenements,
and grimy kids who curse with the pungency
of the odor of gas. You've got America, boy.

Sketch in the river, and barges,
all dirty and slimy.
How do the seagulls stay so white?

And always cawing like little mad geniuses?
You've got the kind of living
that makes the kind of thinking we do:
gaswork smokestacks whistle tooting wisecracks.

They don't come because we like it that way,
but because we find it outside our window every
            morning,
in soot on the furniture,
and trucks carrying coal for gas,
the kid hot after the ball under the wheel.
He gets it over the belly, alright.
He lies there.

So the kids keep tossing the ball around
after the funeral.
So the cops keep chasing them,
so the mamas keep hollering,
and papa flings his newspaper outward,
in disgust with discipline.

That's the kind of poetry which bases itself upon the
world outside, the world around us, and it's really a so-
cial statement. This kind of poetry can't ever go beyond
being a social statement. When social statements are
made, they're made; that's it. But if you keep seeing life
differently with the passing of time and events, your so-
cial statements tend to get confused with one another
and dilute each other. The statement in "Get the Gas-
works" is one I wouldn't make today—about looking
around at the world, looking exactly at the scene. I
wouldn't see it any longer the way I did, nowhere near
it. I'd see it as radically different. How I would see it
now is as a life that people have chosen to live. Poor
people think of themselves as poor, and that's how they
want to live, finally, because they're afraid to live any
other way. Bernard Shaw said that many times. Poor
people are criminal in that sense—that they lose faith in
themselves, faith in the world around them, and they

stay in their ghettos, they stay in their slums. They're afraid to emerge. When social workers from outside come to try and help them, it takes an awful amount of work and persistance on the part of those workers to bring these people out of their poverty and out of their selfin-flicted sense of inferiority. So I would see the whole thing differently if I were to write the poem now, and that new version placed beside the original version—they wouldn't add up quite right. They wouldn't add up to a statement which I could feel satisfied with as a final statement. Well, then there's another way of looking at poetry, altogether differently. Let me read you this next one; it's called "Waiting Inside." Notice that this is no longer written with figures of speech or actual facts. It's almost like statement poetry because I'm working from inside mainly.

Waiting Inside

I protest my isolation
but protest is a mark of my defeat,
even as I write.
          Being a victim,
I am an accuser. Being human,
others feel my fallen weight
upon their thoughts and are oppressed—
as I am, their guilt unlike mine
and unrelated and without hope in it
of change for me.
          Guilty, my oppressor
and I go separate ways
though we could relieve each other
by going together, as Whitman wrote,
with our arms around each other's waists,
in support.

Now notice how it ends in a hope, in a wish, in a vision, should I say? That's a different kind of statement about poetry. There is a series of poems I wrote about trying to define poetry as a way of life, trying to define the nature of poetry. This one is called "Feeling with My Hands"—it's a little different.

Feeling with My Hands

Will this poem be able to think and breathe
and have sex? Will it be able
to lift a finger to call a waiter
for the menu? Will it have hopes
of a future life? Will it have friends
among other poems? Oh yes, will it
be able to write other poems?

I do not want it to rest on its merits.
I want others to look through it
and see me breathing and taking food
and embracing my wife, telling her
she has lovely teeth. This poem
should have an erection and everywhere
should say hello and be a friend
and not hesitate to tell other poems
what it thinks about them. Be pleasant
but be truthful. Be happy but fear not death.
Here it is and I am still talking
and feeling with my hands.

That's a radically different poem—as opposed to the early one, "Get the Gasworks," an altogether different version of what poetry is about.

1976

An Interview
With Richard Jackson and Michael Panori

In your Notebooks *you talk about "seeing everything as a flat surface," referring both to a style and a perceptual mode. You say, "I look back on my style of work and realize that here is only brightness and a certain hardness that comes from light shining on a thing constantly from all sides." Now over the years the notion of darkness has entered your poems more frequently, and you still retain much of the flat style, what Barthes calls "neutral writing," so that the darkness too seems to be a surface. The title* Tread the Dark, *from your last book, suggests this. But sometimes, as in the poem "For Stephen Mooney," the darkness seems more murky, less substantial, less a surface thing.*

In a way, of course, the darkness is a surface. I also think of it as a hard object which you have to go through—it's penetrable. It is the environment that surrounds you and you are in its depths. So you are right in seeing the duality. Sometimes the dark is set off against light, suggesting something like, say, the physical as opposed to the nonphysical. Now in the poem you refer to, the physical presence of the man in the universe is a light, since he is a conscious being, but he could also be the dark generating itself as a conscious object. In a sense, we are an emergent factor from the dark, and what is beyond our consciousness is the unknown, the dark. That doesn't mean the dark is something fearful; it can be something very exciting, the sense of the unexpected. It is our existence; we are perpetually in the dark. Even now, here, we don't even know what we are going to say next.

In my own poetry I can only speak for my own consciousness. It may be that my subconscious rises to a conscious state in writing. I feel myself always in touch with impulses and unformed ideas within me, and when they are framed, articulated, I consider them as breaking to the surface. I don't deliberately search for an unconscious stream; I want everything to finally be on a surface. To bring things to the surface is what it means to live in a consciousness about things.

There's a dialectic of light and dark, then, a balance of inner and outer?

Yes, one doesn't exist without the other; that is true on the level of physics as well as metaphysics. I've thought of myself as mediating the two. I try to reflect simultaneously in my work both the light and the dark. I think there is a quality of ambiguity in the work, an openness. That is, there can be no ending; the light and the dark are constantly merging into one another. And so the poem can't just come to a stop, a finality.

I think a good deal of the open-ended quality of your work is particularly evident in the prose poems in Tread the Dark. *They seem to be more interrogative in mood. In number 9 you end, "I want to call all this the reality. And I must settle for a question." That pretty much seems to define their mode for me.*

That's fairly accurate, though at their centers they are very skeptical questions. It is curious how they have developed. About ten years ago, the free verse lyric was becoming a mannerism, becoming part of "traditional" poetry, as it could not have been called twenty years ago. The short poem method was producing a metaphoric free verse poem focusing on an image. It was becoming too easy, too automatic, and finally too restricting. So I broke away into the prose poem to give more emphasis to the intellect, to the search, to the mind, to thought rather than only feeling, only the image. I couldn't say enough in the short poem; I didn't want to be locked into a metaphor or image, but to go beyond them. I wanted the metaphors to be under my control, I wanted to be in control of the form, to play with the possibilities without having to observe line lengths. The emphasis now fell on developing the metaphor along with an analysis of the metaphor. The point was to analyze the metaphor for what it could give beyond its simple statement. So yes, that gives it the nature of an inquiry; it is constant inquiry.

How have these developed, and the "traditional" poems too? What has the inquiry led you to recently?

A review of the last book called the poems "lyrical meditations," and I think that is accurate. They combine the analytic and the lyrical. But, to me, that is already something I don't want to do. I can't raise questions any more; I want to answer them.

In Tread the Dark *you have a poem that begins, "To look for meaning is as foolish as to find it." It describes a sea shell found on the shore, and the process of examin-*

ing it for a moment is compared to thinking, "So / that thought itself must pause, / holding the shell lightly, / letting it go lightly." Even back fifteen years in the Notebooks, *you say, "It's wrong to read into nature meanings that are not there. All nature should be treated simply as phenomena, happenings, and all happenings treated simply as to their movements." So I want to ask about the nature of "answers" that you would find, the nature of meaning, really. Is it momentary, like the dropped shell? To what degree is it separate from our own subjectivity, or part of it?*

Meaning changes with circumstance. You can read Spinoza today with a meaning he never intended. We produce Shakespeare today in a way he never could have conceived. Meaning is totally relative. As long as language retains its basis in contemporary reality, it is a changing thing. The meanings of things then become lost in this change. A friend of mine, a Chinese scholar, will translate Chinese poems that cannot be translated into their original meanings any longer. The problem is not just with the language because, though he's lucky to know Mandarin, there are still nuances, inflections, intimacies, peculiar details of the historical period that do not cross over. They don't exist. But he has his own reality that the poem must adapt to.

I think of Shelley's statement in the Defense: *"All high poetry is infinite; it is as the first acorn, which contained all oaks potentially. Veil after veil may be undrawn . . . and after one person of one age has exhausted all its diverse effluence which their peculiar relations enable them to share, another and another succeeds, and new relations are ever developed."*

I have a good example. I recently saw a show at the Museum of Natural History about some people who were living 30,000 years ago. Their images, artifacts, drawings of men and women are amazingly like ours, and with a degree of sophistication amazingly like Picasso's. But these things have different meanings for us than they did for them. We have applied another view, an aesthetic one. Perhaps for them the meaning was cultural or religious, or perhaps they did combine the aesthetic with other meanings.

Are there limits to what things can mean? I'm thinking of your poem "The Question," where you ask, as you dream you are flying above the city, "if I say the people are bacteria/who will deny it?" You commented elsewhere that you like Jackson Mac Low's experiments with a poetry of meaninglessness.

Well, the character in "The Question" is creating his own reality, but he still has to come down sometime, as the end of the poem suggests. The reality is what we all participate in, our culture that we draw from. Even when you withdraw from it there is an emotional and mental attachment. In the background is our culture with its different thought habits. Reality according to the poem is that which you are in at the moment. By meaninglessness, I meant in relation to a single meaning, a single reality. I don't mean that an object has no meaning, but that the meaning we give it is of the moment, while we are in communication with it.

Related to what we have been discussing is a certain primacy you give to the moment, the now. In the Note-books *you say, "The highest poetry recreates the reality of the moment and in recreating assures itself of immortality, because it is in the process of recreating that poetry is most akin to reality."*

Time is the body, the body is the poem. I don't see time in a classical sense. Recent scientific theory is correct—time and space are the same thing, and space is physical. We're space. Space lengthens, time lengthens. If time is the body, then the body is of every moment, a constant process. So I try analogously in my poems to create the moment as a bodily thing, as a moment of the body. Now I don't think of the body as merely physical; isolated from intelligence and feelings, it is not human. The poem is a consciousness of the author which also involves a sense of the body within his total meaning for the poem. The lines, the language, the rhythm, the syntax should recreate the physicality of the body at the same time they are being employed to create an insight, an idea.

As you say in another Notebook *entry, "No ideas but in things and things die, with their ideas," in a parodic extension of Williams's statement. The poem, you suggest, is like an echo, a footprint—"the voice of a bird echoing after its silence and even death." How is this sort of echo through time related to the moment?*

The poems that I write are really episodes or parts of an ongoing long poem that will never end. It can't end because the body of the universe doesn't end. To establish a sense of the physical in language is to identify with everything that is around you that will always go on, will always be physical. In everything I write I try to celebrate the physical. It's the idea that changes more than the physical. That's where meaning is so relative, to go back to what we were saying before.

How does this notion of celebration relate to the dark, to the "tragic" vision you have identified in your own work? I remember a stunning passage in the Notebooks *that describes the way the universe is expanding, creating greater distances, more emptiness, more nothingness. Ironically, it is as if Emerson's transcendent circles were being hollowed out.*

I think I'll have to go back to my feelings about Whitman. I have a lengthy article, written some time ago, where I talk about my total faith in the ability of Whitman's work to turn people around and give them fellowship, and perhaps ameliorate some of the harsh conditions we live in. It took me a long time to realize this whole need for fellowship was not going to be brought about by his poetry and prose. Still, you don't want to give up on such an idea. So I said, if it is not going to work out in the affirmative, at least let us communicate that we can't have fellowship. At least that is a human and civilizing thing to do. That's the tragic aspect of the vision. Everything I've gained from Whitman can be seen in this negative sense. That is, I'm reflecting his concept of transcendence, his concept of progress toward man's total communal society. What I retain from him is his ability to remain open to everything, and therefore reflecting given forms in poetry and living. His idea is to make life for yourself rather than have life make you, and that is enough to gain from any poet.

Sometimes that self you are trying to make seems threatened with an inwardness in Tread the Dark *which leads to a kind of terror. In poem 51 you confront a door be-hind which may stand some other fearful self. "The Two Selves" also seems to deal with the problem, though in a different way. By the end of the book, these selves, even the whole problem, seems to have been shucked off. The dark has become light, to use the earlier metaphor.*

It's that I've gone past that stage. It seems to me now to be basically a middle-class problem, the problem of the person who serves himself through society, remains iso-lated, and then, maybe, finally confronts himself as iso-lated even from himself. We have to serve society through ourselves. This is what the poet should do, however limited that service is in our present society. We define ourselves through others. So I don't personally have a sense of loss of identity. If I do question my identity, it is to question myself as a human being in relation to a tree, or the sea—it's to know myself as a human being, as a being in life, and to communicate that to others. In "The Two Selves" I meant the question in a physical sense—what was I before and after I was born? Did I ever know myself at the time of my birth? The poem, as we said earlier, brings these things to the surface, to communicate them to others, to share our identity with others, to have a sense of community.

Would you say your vision has become more optimistic? Certainly it is at least more stoical. In the poem "Ex-plorer," using the metaphor of mountain climbing, you say, "I am about to begin," and then, "My joy is in the trees and grass . . ." and "My joy is skyward," and finally, end the poem with "I am the joyful man."

I think I am going in a direction that is, ironically, the opposite of what Robert Bly, a poet I have tremendous respect for, is recently doing. From my conversations with him, I begin to sense he feels that transcendence has its own limitation; he's starting to go below the surface where the quirkiness of individuals lies, not their general human consciousness. I want to see if there's a possibility of transcendence, though certainly not in any Emersonian sense. I hope to do something different in the next book, to say yes to a lot of things. Perhaps I've been saying no too long.

1978

An Interview
With Gerard Malanga

Do you consider yourself vulnerable?

Vulnerable, damn right. I think it's quite typical of me, but the fear of being vulnerable prompts me into bringing myself forward. It's like being on the battlefield. As you engage in battle, you begin to feel fear, but as you make contact with the enemy, he's almost your friend because he's reducing the fear to excitement and participation. In *Facing the Tree* there's one poem about Croatian guerrillas who are being executed, and they keep identifying with the executioner. It's strange. It's terribly ironical.

The vulnerability in your poems—especially in those instances where you show your anger—I'm speaking specifically of poems like "Emergency Clinic," "To Nowhere," "Beautiful and Kind," "The Boss," and "Envoy"—do you feel a danger in having your vulnerability misunderstood?

I couldn't care less. This is what I have to feel, this is what I have to write. This is the life, this is the life. I'm living it.

Visceral is a term, that might be appropriate in describing your poetry. Do you feel it's an accurate description?

Very much so. My poetry is a gut reaction. I've lived a gut life for so many years, and I guess I still do. When we talk of the gut, I mean literally sometimes being worried where I'm going to get the money for the next rent. Always living on the edge.

Anthony Burgess said "The scientific approach to life is not really appropriate to states of visceral anguish. . . ."

That's very good. Visceral anguish is really survivor's experience, he who fights his way back from the edge of a cliff or burrows his way out of a locked cage, out of the coal mine—a perpetual struggle.

What is the worst thing that could happen to you?

Well—losing my job, being out of money. Problems of love, problems of human relationships are secondary. Emotional problems have a way of resolving themselves.

You write in the Notebooks *that pain is your favorite subject. Do you still believe that?*

I probably have passed that point in my life. Things have changed for me. And I don't intend to go on living a life of pain and celebrating pain. I really have experienced a tremendous joy in the last three years. I've been fantastically happy in long spurts. This is something I haven't had for many years.

Over the years, you seem to have become more preoccupied with prose poems. Does this visual change in your work correspond to the way you've changed your life? Have you become impatient, or more patient with yourself?

Well, the lyric has limitations. I've found myself impatient with the lyric form. And that's the reason I changed my style—a rebellion against the—traditional, contemporary, lyric form, of, say, William Carlos Williams. I had had it that way. I found my language was responding to the form rather than to my sensibilities. I was getting a little too self-conscious about it. So I decided to cut loose and give emphasis to the imagination rather than to the line. By imagination I mean also the intelligence within the imagination, giving the intelligence its opportunity to explore the imagination as far as it will *go*. Of course it has a form, but it's a form which constantly renews itself because the intelligence is restless. Emotions tend to repeat themselves over and over again, whereas the intelligence is constantly renewing itself, recreating itself. Therefore, I feel in the prose poems the emphasis is on the intelligence with an undercurrent of emotion. In the lyric form the emphasis was on the emotion and the intellect was the undercurrent. I'm also following Pound's rule, that poetry should be as good as good prose. That it's a vernacular, colloquial thing, and vernacular, colloquial doesn't sing—it talks. If you want to sing, then you write an elevated line, an elevated language. Occasionally, I'll do that. There are moments, but, on the whole, the contemporary tradition is talking. If that's the case, then why not come out and use the prose line?

When you started to write, who were your chief influences?

At first I was very pleased to model myself on Hart Crane. But then I knew I wasn't a Crane temperament; I felt much more closely aligned with Whitman, so I began to model myself on him. Then I found that I couldn't quite grasp the Whitman thing because he was just a little too euphoric for me. So I went away from him and I went to Williams. Williams repelled me at first. He repelled me because he was so—I felt he was so literal, so prosy. Where is the poetry in all this?, I kept thinking. All the praise he was getting from people had me hanging on the ropes. I said, "I've got to come back and read him again." So I kept going back and reading him. I was finding myself in experiences which were shockingly similar to the experiences he was recounting in his work. When I started to write these experiences, I saw that I was using his techniques. There was no other choice. But then, my life diverged from his in many respects. First of all, he was a physician. My life-style went in the opposite direction. So I began to reshape the technique according to *my* life-style. Then I met César Vallejo on the page and, boy, he flipped me out! Then, I said, "I'm going to let loose."

Who have been some of your other influences?

I learned the surrealist technique from Russell Edson. Before I read him I had made a jab at surrealist poetry and I dropped it very quickly, because my life became much too complicated and in need of direct confrontation to keep it simple. Later on I was reminded of my past attempts when I read Edson. I said, "Gee, I must try it again." Then, as I said, Vallejo was very important to me, the intellectualization of *states of being* that I think characterizes his work. The extraordinary combination of the guts and the mind—how they get together and inform one another. He's a metaphysical poet. By metaphysical, I mean he's a man who's constantly seeking values. Neruda, too—the whole Spanish school of poetry gave me much to think about. They drew me away from the Whitman tradition and I thought myself freer—freed of the Whitman tradition.

Yet you're often characterized as the son of Whitman and Williams.

I know, but I don't believe it altogether. I have a lot of bizarre, surrealistic, macabre images at work in my head. The ill curse of contemporary life. I think if Williams were alive today, he would've gone in that direction. As for Whitman, if you take him seriously you have to swallow the whole bit about man's divine origins and all men being equal. I reject that. I don't see it in practice, therefore it doesn't exist for me. It's purely an idea, a vision of the future. History is now, *this is it!* Not what's going to happen.

So, you don't use Whitmanesque techniques any more.

I still use some of his repetition, parallel structures, chanting, incantatory style, but it's more evident in my earlier work. It grows much tighter and more intellectual, more imagistic with the years because of my study of men like Neruda, Vallejo, Machado, and the French poets.

When you came upon the surrealist poets did you feel that the Whitman tradition had limitations for you that forced you to move on to the surrealist poets?

The limitation in the Whitman tradition was its openness to everything at a time when it seemed wrong to be open to everything. That is, to accept evil, the kind of evil that was going on, to believe that it could be transcended or transformed or used. I didn't think that any of this could happen. The pivot really is my turning toward the existentialist movement. I felt man ought to judge himself—there was no one to appeal to, contrary to Whitman's work. That is to say that there is a final arbiter in life. I don't think so. An arbiter beyond the personal, beyond the individual—I don't believe it. But Whitman tried to straddle two concepts: the individual as a unique person with a strength of his own and the concept that beyond the individual since he was of a divine source, was still a greater force than he toward which he was progressing to perfect himself. I had to throw all that out; I was left with the individual. That was it, which unraveled the whole Whitman tradition for me. Therefore, I had to turn to other sources and other sensibilities. These were men like Rimbaud and Baudelaire who were very important to me—Williams and the Spanish poets who dealt with pain, from suffering, from severe deprivation: mental, physical, social, universal. Yet they sought to expand their world. They sought to include the entire world in their pain and suffering and their anguish toward a freer life. The kind that Whitman sought for—the kind that Whitman thought he had. In other words, they were going through the door of life, toward Whitman, whereas Whitman *thought* he had opened the front door.

A Mexican writer José Gaos was quoted in Octavio Paz's beautiful book The Bow and the Lyre *as saying "As soon as a man enters life he is already old enough to die."*

That's good. When you assume that knowledge you begin to live a very vital life, because everything you do is in the background of immortality. The background is the immortality of death. That's when you can say you are a man in the full sense of the word. You've become an existentialist. That's what it's all about.

How old were you when you first began writing?

About sixteen when I realized that I had some kind of a gift.

Were you excited because all of a sudden you realized that you were dealing with a secret language?

No. I was able to make things vivid on the page. I could recreate, I could bring life to a page. That's what I was thinking about. To see my visions on paper almost exactly as I had visualized them, being read and viewed with pleasure the way I had viewed them myself. That's what amazed me. I didn't *will* myself to become a writer. It was just a natural outgrowth of the pleasure readers got from my work. I wanted to give pleasure and give myself pleasure.

Does it help you as a writer to go for long periods without sex?

Sexuality, in itself, is quite a distraction. It's an art in itself. It requires a tremendous amount of concentration and delicacy and nuance, and that takes a lot of practice—knowing the other person. If your time is limited, that *really* can cut into your writing. It's really a common problem. Our profession requires almost a total concentration of personality and the moment you start to divert yourself, you begin to lose your grip and you drift, and you become quite irritable about it, too.

In the Notebooks *you say: "Being a poet is to know*

you do not exist by poetry." What does that mean?

I guess, at some point you have got to think that you exist for poetry. But if you remove love from your life or you remove, say, the financial security from your life, then you know that poetry plays a very minor role. This is the age of survival. That's the point. If life wasn't so dangerous, and we had a stable form of society, then I suppose poetry would play a more prominent role. When did I say that, by the way?

1964.

Well, I was going through some real problems then. Very heavy financial burdens. My business had collapsed. Not "my" business, the family business. I had sold it in 1962, after my father's death, I left myself out on a limb. I sold it for nothing! All I wanted was to get free of the whole entanglement.

You seem profoundly energetic as a teacher of other poets, and also prolific as a poet in your own right. What is the relation between these activities?

Teaching poetry has stimulated me no end. At the beginning it was virtually an explosive experience! Because, as I had to get up there and discuss poetry, I was really, finally, articulating ideas that had remained unsaid in my mind. The whole thing illuminated my past and my present, and I found myself taking tremendous leaps forward as a writer.

How do you feel when someone imitates you?

I'm uneasy.

When you started writing poetry, were you interested in something like what John Wieners calls "the fellowship of poets"? Were you eager to meet a lot of poets?

Very much so. I thought poets would be the ideal candidates for a community of spirits. I still had the Whitman thing in me. The more I became familiar with poets, the more I recognized that they were limited human beings, like myself. I was extremely excited to see how different they were from me, which accounted for differences in their poetry, too. So, I'm still interested in meeting poets. I like to talk with them. I like to feel them out. I like to read their work. But I'm not searching for myself in their work; I'm searching for something which affirms differences—creative differences—between us.

Do you ever feel lonely?

Oh sure. I'm lonely most of the time. I'm always after company. I guess when I'm writing I feel I've suddenly made company with myself. You become your own guest.

Or your own audience.

Yeah. And that's fine. That's very nice. Out of a day, that represents three or four hours at the most. There are times when I can find myself in a book, too, for two or three hours, but afterward I have such an urge to go out and reach for other people. Very often they're not around. There's also a metaphysical loneliness. We all feel it. The burden of living one's own life is experiencing sensations that no one else can share. You take a step in a house, you start moving around the house, no one else moves with you. You're walking by yourself.

I take it you're living alone?

Yeah.

Do you prefer living alone, or would you rather have someone living with you?

I'd like to have someone living with me. My family is out in East Hampton. We're separated for practical reasons. I have my work here; my office, my schoolwork. I travel out there on weekends, but when I'm there I get very restless because it's a totally isolated area. I've lived long enough in the country; I've done some nice things on the life lived among trees and rabbits and fox and geese—but now I want to come back and hear the gunfire and watch drunks vomiting in the street and hear the buses roaring on the avenue. Actually, I'm getting to the point, living here by myself, of getting used to it. I'm used to living in a domestic environment, with a family—all my life. Brought up—surrounded by family. So this is the first time I ever pitched myself into this sort of thing. When I left my parents' home I got myself a small apartment in New York, in the Village, and I started housekeeping. But then I went out hunting for women—you know, someone to share my life with me. Now it's all settled—I'm not looking.

Right, because you know that the options are there. Where in the country there aren't that many options on that kind of social level. Also, one never finds what one is looking for. You have to stop looking—stop searching, in order to allow for recognition of a person or object in your life without having to debate between alternatives.

Who needs it? Sex is fine in its place.

What's better than sex?

Jeez, I'm going to spend my whole life thinking about that one! That's a hard subject—that's a hard question to answer. Well, what do you think is better than sex?

Not thinking about sex; but to be active in whatever your commitment is in your life, like being a poet, for instance.

It's a different degree of tension, different degree of concentration, different order of experience, different order of passion. It's visceral. Sex is a tremendous investment of visceral experience. The whole body goes into it. And you're aware of your whole body being into it; even vocally, you are participating. Whereas, in the writing, in your art—especially for a poet—it's mainly mental. So, you don't have that same degree of passion, and it's a different kind of passion; intellectual, I suppose. Creatively—an imaginative passion. Sex is itself and there's nothing to compare it with.

Back to the Notebooks, *again, you speak quite a bit about isolation. Do you feel more or less isolated now than at the beginning of your career as a poet?*

Much less isolated now. I know there are people out in the world who have read my work and who know what I'm doing.

In the past you were isolated, culturally from your contemporaries. How do you account for this?

When the New Criticism was in ascendence in the 1940s, and I was also isolated from the proletarian school of the 1930s, because it was so totally ideological—the

Communist party, the War Poets. I didn't go to war. I was married and I was deferred for quite some time. When the war was coming to a conclusion I was called up, but I had some kind of heart murmur. The Japanese attack, the Nazi horror, the Italian fiasco—none of this really affected me. I was so deeply involved, with my personal domestic relationships even in those years. Since I did feel myself to be a very private man, it explains why I had an antipathy toward the school of proletarian poetry in the 1930s, and why, in turn, I had antipathy toward the whole school of New Criticism. The sort of poetry they were writing was metaphysical in the most tenuous sense; they were philosophically oriented and in their work they began with a principle or a hypothesis and then tried to create the poem from either one. Whereas, I was deriving my poetry directly from life experience. In that sense I was anticipating the poetry of the 1960s and the 1970s. So, I was isolated for a good many years, because I was such a *personal* guy. It was only in the early 1960s that poets began to flourish within themselves as the so-called confessional poets, but I wasn't a confessional poet either.

In a sense, you were, but not in a pretentious sense.

No, I wasn't flagellating myself or exposing my weaknesses just to show how weak a person I was like Randall Jarrell and Robert Lowell and Sylvia Plath.

Your situation is very unique. Is there another poet that is similar to you?

Of my generation? No.

Were poets like Meredith and William Jay Smith and Jarrell and Eberhart aware of your presence?

Jarrell wrote a favorable, very short review of my work. He called me a street Sophocles or something like that because I would take the theme of *Hamlet* or the theme of *Oedipus* and put it in the language of the living room, the language of ordinary conversation. To him, that was remarkable. Otherwise, I was a total nonentity.

You went your own way, you were your own man, your own poet.

Right. Really, I'd been formed much earlier in my life by the experiences in my parents' home. What I saw there left its mark upon me ever since. I saw how important it was to maintain personal initiative, to remain an individual. Because with my parents I was always in the precarious position of being submerged in their interests and subjected to their manipulations. I had to fight it and discover myself—discover myself through this conflict. I extricated myself from their demands on me. That is the traumatic experience I think I brought into my poetry that was so different from everyone else. I found it very difficult to be accepted by magazines in those years. The styles were formed in schools, you see, and they had to be recognizably so.

And the WPA was obviously one particular school.

It was a school in itself. Strangely enough, I wrote very little about my WPA experiences—almost nothing. I had some remarkable experiences on the WPA, and on Relief, and I never got to writing about it because I felt to do so would violate my individual integrity. I must have been terribly neurotic about it.

There were instances—moments or topics—in the Notebooks *where I wished you would have elaborated more, such as the passage where you say: "What is it about my life I don't like? It is the lack of more fame, the uses of one's self that come from it, the sense of belonging."*

What an awfully self-involved person that is!

Was it because you were not recognized or famous that you felt isolated?

Well, in order to be famous, you have to write a poetry that's accepted by people whose opinions you respect. In the early periods I was trying to do that. But after I had written the kind of poetry *I thought* deserved the respect and the attention of people whose opinions *I* respected, I discovered, to my dismay, that I was writing a kind of poetry which really did not relate to the taste or the interests of my generation in any way!

Are you interested in fame or in being famous?

No, I just want to be useful. To me, fame means contributing. Giving the community something helpful.

A nourishment.

That's all, and being nourished back in return. Giving it love and getting love in return. To stand apart on some platform and have people wave their little white handkerchiefs at you? That's horseshit. That's movie idolatry.

In your opinion, who were the prominent poets of your generation?

Lowell, Jarrell, and Berryman. I was divided from all of them because my experiences were not their experiences.

My style and my life-style are altogether different from theirs. The war psychology those guys brought home was such a strong social bind on them; they couldn't get away from it. A guy like Jarrell made a deliberate effort after returning from the war to be personal in his world and it just wasn't convincing on that level. He couldn't get into the adult stage of his life. Berryman made a very slight attempt to reach out to me—we met at a party—a reception for, I think, Edwin Honig and his wife. That was more or less at the beginning of Berryman's career. I think he had just completed *Homage to Mistress Bradstreet*. At the party he called me over and we talked briefly, less than one minute, and I just sort of clammed up. I wasn't interested, because that poem didn't interest me. It was highly artificial to me, tremendously willed artifice, and I was turned off by it. That explains a lot of my isolation, you know. Generally, generations stick together and they take to each other and they help promote each other. I didn't experience that, though the others promoted each other a great deal. The generation that followed them began to take notice of me. The younger generation. The generation of Harvey Shapiro.

Well, has your current fame altered your sense of vocation?

No, I'm still struggling to be the guy I dreamt I was going to be when I was a child. That dream—I don't think I am anywhere near it, to be the exponent of the national sensibility, whatever that is. No, the vocation of writing poetry means remaining a private poet. When I write my political poetry it's as a private citizen. Fame hasn't changed much, except that I have a wider and heavier correspondence than I ever had before. I may have to get an answering service. And the fact that I can help edit an important magazine like the *American Poetry Review* (*APR*) is something I'm rather grateful for. [As of late 1976, he is no longer an editor.]

Why did Williams mean so much to you?

Well, he was a poet of national reputation who came out in the *New York Times* with a review of my first book to call it a potential national best-seller, strangely enough. I felt I was confirmed as a poet. From then on I could feed on that in a dry season, and I fed on it for many years. It watered my desert, my loneliness, for a long time.

In what way was he useful to you that was different from other poets?

He was useful in his being present, on the scene—in this country as a *person*. Without him, American poetry was impoverished for me.

But he was also getting a lot of negative feed-back.

That's right. This is what astonished me, finally, when I began to recognize that he too was almost as isolated as I. Nevertheless, he was *somebody*. He was respected, endemic to American poetry. He represented the American grain. He made life important.

Did you feel that certain poets refused to acknowledge you as poet because of your allegiance to Williams?

I think that happened. Oscar Williams tried to cultivate my friendship at one point. I was witness to a confrontation that he had with Williams one day, and Oscar

Williams was so nasty and insulting to William Carlos Williams. Williams was sitting there very patiently smiling at this guy, not letting himself lose his temper, but Oscar was like a buzzing fly diving in on him. I developed an intense dislike for Oscar Williams after that. That immediately disenfranchised me from the other poets he was publishing and left me out of his anthologies forever.

So, you felt even more isolated for supporting Williams?

I think there was an intensification of my isolation as a result of my allegiance to Williams, yes. Of course, it was happening anyway. I couldn't publish in *Poetry* or *Accent*. The stuff was automatically sent back. That was the school of New Criticism. I wanted to be part of the establishment. I thought the establishment could have some variety within itself—in the Whitman spirit. Of course, I should have known better. Ransom was a gentleman and not a Whitmanite. A gentleman that preferred—

—Tea and biscuits.

Yeah.

So, the critics had a headlock on the scene?

Total censorship.

How would you evaluate Lowell's influence?

When Lowell came along, he—his style—completely cornered the market in magazines like *Partisan Review,* the *Nation,* the *New Republic,* the *Atlantic Monthly* and *Harper's.* Most of us were under the shadow of his fame. Those of us who couldn't conform to that kind of writing were shuttled off into the little out-of-the-way magazines.

But he was a breath of fresh air.

Oh, yes. His early work is exceptionally good. So he was a double-barreled power, a genuine poet whose influence blanketed the entire northern sector.

He also helped to carry certain poets, like Delmore Schwartz.

He nurtured them. But that's past now. Passed into the shadows. The whole school has just evaporated.

How did Lowell's influence affect Williams's influence?

At the time Lowell's prominence in the northern sector was tremendously damaging to Williams's literary influence. Now, to Lowell's credit, he was able to see into the work of Williams. Lowell became a very good friend of his, and Williams learned to tolerate him and became quite affectionate. So, when Lowell published *Life Studies,* the influence of Williams was marked.

Getting back to you, to what do you attribute your survival during this long, lonely, struggling period of isolation?

Well, I had a friend here and a friend there and my wife was very strongly in my favor, which was great. She worked with me closely on my poems.

Is it possible for you to specify some of the things Williams enabled you to guard against?

Against a romantic view of life. Against elevated language. Against trying to make a leap into something which didn't exist. He taught me to guard against being dogmatic, didactic, opinionated. He taught me to stay within the circumference of the experience. If you know your limitations and cultivate these limitations to their limits, that will extend you into the very next area which you may not be able to get into thoroughly, but at least you'll be anticipating something that goes beyond your limitations.

On page 84 in the Notebooks, *which is 1954, you say: "I like to take refuge in the belief that I share a fault common to all poets today. I would assume none is adequately educated and trained as poet for the job." What did you mean by that?*

Well, by comparison with Dante, who I looked up to reverentially. He was so deeply learned in the Catholic dogma, particularly in the work of Aquinas, in the structure of heaven and hell, that were part of the whole tradition of those years—and, looking around the contemporary scene, we don't have a philosophy that could really give us that kind of a definitive, encompassing view of life. Dante wrote out of a philosophical premise, while being very deeply personal in doing it. We can only write experientially and discover our philosophy through our experiences. After Dante, you say to yourself that what we're missing is that prime ingredient, that essential ingredient, the philosophical definitiveness or view of life that he had. He was given it. He lived in a tradition. This was life, as he knew it, and there was no other choice. We have proliferated all over the place. We're so intellectually in conflict with ourselves and with the times that the philosophy we do get into our work is the philosophy of conflict, the philosophy of compromise, of indecisiveness, contradiction, and paradox. It's just titanic, the problem we have.

Can we return to the past and get very personal. In the Notebooks, *you say that you met with resistance from your father about your poetry.*

Yes, very strong resistance. It was harrowing, to say the least. I began working for him about six months after I graduated from high school; I was about eighteen and a half, with no job and no prospect of a job. This was deep in the Depression, 1932 going on 1933. Well, I had no choice. I tried staying home for a while and writing. I had the illusion that if I wrote the great short story, I would make my whole family rich. I was aiming at the *Saturday Evening Post,* and I wrote a story about a couple that meets on a transatlantic liner, they fall in love and get married. She was rich. That whole number. He was a writer. Writing in big, romantic slashes. Well, it got turned down, of course. So, I realized that I wasn't going to make the family fortune as a writer. That sort of collapsed my resistance toward my parents. They were trying to be very patient with me. They were in very desperate financial straits at that time. The old man was living on a quarter a day! You could have a bowl of soup for ten cents, and you could have a roll and butter for a nickel, and I suppose the other ten cents went for goodies of some kind. Well, when he came home he was desperately tired. I could see his whole appearance changing under the circumstances; he became quite gaunt. But I absolutely had to be a writer. My old man had a little insight into these things. He came from Russia and loved Russian literature. He had books at home. That was during his period as a worker. He was quite a man, quite an affable guy; very sociable and very loving. But somehow he was influenced by his brother, who was rather wealthy, to become an enterprising business-man and he changed. When he was younger he told me stories by Dostoevsky and others which I found fasci-nating. He had such a great *love* for these writers that I said, "I must emulate them because I want that kind of a love from my father!"

In the long run, it was a reaction that worked against you?

Right. He humored me for a while, for six months, but I had no skill at that kind of *Saturday Evening Post* crap. Well, bite the bullet; I had to go to work. *That's* when the real tension started between us. We fought like cat and dog. Many a time I thought I was going to kill him; many a time I thought he was going to kill me. It was awful. Very often I'd leave the shop when everyone else would be working overtime. I'd try to eat and rest and get my strength together to write. He'd come home at eight o'clock and say, "Where is that bastard?! Where's that son-of-a-bitch!?" It really broke my heart because I *knew* how much he loved me.

What did your job consist of?

The business was a pamphlet bindery—machine work—or I had to push carts through the streets downtown, just above Canal Street. That's how I became acquainted with the Village: loading the pushcart and hauling it over to the printer. I was in the business on and off. I'd run away. I tried to join the Army; the Army turned me down. Then one day I said, "I'm finished, I'm never coming back again." I had exactly ten cents in my pocket. I took the train to Borough Hall in Brooklyn;

I had heard that boys would gather around the fountain there and form groups, then they'd go out through the country, looking for jobs or taking freight trains—anything to get away. I decided I was going to do that. I could see they were a tough bunch of bastards; very hardened, cruel, cynical guys. They'd been through much worse than I had. They had no good clothes on; I was fairly well-dressed. They scared me. "Christ, get in with these guys, I'm going to be really finished! Where's my career as a writer?" I had spent five cents for fare and I'd spent five cents for peanuts. I had no money. So I walked over the Brooklyn Bridge back to the shop. I walked in. The old man turned around and saw me. There was a big grin on his face. He went to the telephone, called my mother and said, "He's here. Your little boy is here." So that fixed me for about a year. I ground it out from eight in the morning until five, five-thirty, working and trying to write at night. It was awful. But I wrote.

What characteristics have you inherited from your parents?

My mother's stubborn pride and my father's highly mercurial temperament. Within a half an hour he could show you seven different sides of himself: very excited, or very warm, or very angry, or very jovial. He had a creative temperament. My mother had a staunch capacity to stick with something—stay with it and endure it. I have that very much, too. She was very stoic, a very strong woman! The post in the house—you know, the anchor. She kept the whole thing together. From her I learned how to handle domestic problems, money, and emotions. I always remind myself of her steadfast, plodding manner in the house to compose myself under stress in my own domestic relationships.

How did you finally get out of that job?

I think it was 1932 or 1933. I'd published a short story that was named on the honor list in the *Best Short Stories of the Year* anthology, and out of the blue I got this letter! The WPA was looking for writers to fill its Writers Project. A godsend!

Could you settle down and work any place in the States other than New York?

I don't think so. I've turned down teaching jobs in Berkeley, Michigan, Kansas; I wouldn't have kept my voice there as a poet.

You're quoted as saying that the writing of a poem is a celebration to you. "the experience of one's everyday life that readers can relate to." Have you found a joy in despair? How can a poem of pain also be a poem of celebration?

Well, there's no suffering without life; there's no life without suffering. Put on the coat of life, and it has two sides to it; it has suffering and joy. It all depends what the weather is. If the weather is joyful, you turn the coat on to the joyful side; if it's full of suffering, you turn it to the suffering side.

When did you begin to recognize this element of celebration in your poetry?

If there was a turning point, it was when my son's breakdown happened. I was ready to give up. But what was I going to give up? I mean, I'd seen the worst already, what worse could there be? He needed me to at least sur-

vive his own ordeal, and I had to stay well. I had to stay
well for my wife's sake, too. You can't go on despairing—
it'll drown you.

There was one very vivid passage in the Notebooks *where
you ran into your son on the street carrying your diaries—*

My notebooks.

—to oblivion.

And I didn't stop him. Amazing. I didn't stop him, be-
cause I felt so sick, so sick of everything already—dumped
them in the Hudson River. I just shrugged and said, "Oh,
he's got the notebooks on him." He even said to me,
"I've got your notebooks in here." He threw away a
couple of years of notebooks. I just shrugged and went
upstairs. He went and dumped them into the Hudson
River.

What's he like, your son?

In a rather crippled way, he's a survivor. It's interesting.
I tend to agree with Laing that the emotionally disturbed
child is simply not bound to the culture and would like
to free himself of the culture, and this is the only means
he has with which to express his independence. We imme-
diately term these people insane, but they're not. They
have created a different order of existence for themselves,
which doesn't have a basis in reality. They can't organize
a society around themselves; they don't have the means
with which to do it. They're powerless, absolutely pow-
erless. They have to be put in a special category, a special
place. My son continues to have hallucinations—different
people, voices—but he's very practical-minded. He knows

that he's getting enough money on SSI (Supplemental Security Income) to cover his expenses; whereas, if he were to go out for a job, he couldn't make any more than that. And he might be in danger of rebelling again and once more become really incapable of handling a job. So, he thought all this out; he decided that this is it, this is what he has to do; he has to stay where he is until he can really recover himself, and integrate with society the way he sees me integrating. I can understand it. I'm quite sure that if he were to drop from SSI and be forced to take a job, he'd crack-up again. Because, to him, society in that sense is worthless, doesn't mean a thing.

How old is he now?

In his thirties.

Has the relationship now improved between you and your son?

Well, I spent thousands and thousands and thousands of dollars on him at one point. I broke myself. He'd come out, go to a psychiatrist. He came out three times—and back three times. So I had no more money. There was nothing left I could do for him. I was trying to be very close to him during that period, but I couldn't penetrate. Couldn't get beyond his hallucinatory states. Or, when he would have that more or less under control with the aid of a doctor and some medicine, he would be quite a tense young man. It would be very hard to take him into my confidence, or he to take me into his confidence. He was just too tense and he'd be very hard in the house. The whole atmosphere of the house would be so charged with his emotion—which couldn't be articulated. He was already twenty-three when my daughter was to be born, and he became violent and we had to get him out of the house again. So that was the extent of our relationship. Today he'll drop up to see me occasionally, but there isn't much that we can say to each other. He's lost contact with his old friends and just maintains relationships with the guys around him who are also from the hospital. They talk about baseball, they ride around in a car occasionally, go see this, go see that, and they talk about their meals—but it's very low level stuff. No intellectual content in his life at all. He avoids it like the plague. So we sit there and we have nothing to say to each other. He has no interest in my work. I don't know, I could talk to him about baseball all the time. Baseball or good food. That's the relationship.

How do you feel about money?

Well, I'm not a Buddha in the sense of sitting under a tree for a thousand years. Who can? The climate doesn't allow for it, anyway. So we need money. We need money for houses and for comforts. To relax.

Are you an impulsive writer, or do you set aside a certain number of hours to write?

I've alternated between being impulsive and scheduled. When I was living out in East Hampton, during the three grants that I was lucky to get, I organized myself on a morning schedule, and, whether I had anything to say or not, I would sit down at the typewriter and slip in a piece of paper there, and I would tell myself there was nothing to write until something finally emerged, and I'd just keep at it for three or four hours. Those were the years when I didn't have to teach; I didn't have any other schedule to keep except my writing schedule, and so a lot of work got produced. Now, trying to keep a schedule these days while teaching—it's impossible! I write when I can.

How do you write?

I write either by typewriter or in the notebook.

Do you work from drafts?

Sure. I get the first idea down as fast as possible. Sometimes it's largely successfully realized, with just a few little things needed here and there. But I'd say just as often I have to fool around with it afterward. Often I want it to grow cold on me so I can go back and become the critic of it. Then, seeing it cold, I see what really emerges and what doesn't, and I can almost instantly supply the needed lines or stanza. In this way I may have three or four poems going at one time.

Do you write a poem straight to its end, or do you write a poem in sections and then proceed to fit the sections together?

Well, the shorter poems I complete. I can go to forty or fifty lines, and then come back to it and see what I could use. There were poems like the "Ritual" poems, which were written in steps and stages. Each one had to be written over a period of several weeks—had to rethink it over and over again. I'll often take a lot of short poems, which might have been written over a period of four or five years, and put them in a sequence. I come back to my subjects, come back to my themes over and over again, and look at them differently as time goes by. There's always a new emphasis.

Do your working habits vary with the nature of the poem?

Oh, yes. Sometimes I can take it quite casually, where I could knock off, say, ten or twelve lines, and just let it rest for a while. At other times, I feel I must go on. I often get an impulse. If I get started on a poem, I feel I must go to the very end of it. I exhaust myself. Say, if it's a thirty or forty line poem I just have to do it! Nothing can stand in the way; but then, often enough, I find that I've gone too far.

How long does it generally take you to finish a poem?

Anywhere from ten minutes to ten hours.

How do you know when a poem's finished; how do you know when to stop writing?

Well, if I feel I'm no longer getting an image, or a metaphor, of what has to be said, or I feel that the cadences are petering out, or that I'm beginning to comment on the poem itself I just drop it. At other times I feel that I may be writing tongue-in-cheek.

In writing a poem, has any one problem given you particular trouble?

Changes in style. When I become conscious of a change in my style, I begin to fluctuate between the new and the old. I have to find a middle path until I'm able to go over entirely in the new direction. For example, in my very earliest writing I was trying to emulate Shelley in denouncing contemporary faults and corruption, quite high-flown in my language. But I found myself growing out of that as my city experience began to grow. I was excited about the city, the tremendous excitement of seeing so many thousands of people on the streets and in buildings, movement everywhere, and I felt very much like Whitman: there was great hope in all this movement. I broke with that finally after a couple of years when I recognized that beneath all this movement and excitement and colorfulness was something very nasty, very vicious, very rough, very ruthless. Well, I felt I just couldn't go back to denouncing. What I did was become very objectivist; I began to do picture writing. I did that for quite some time, and then I had to change because I became tired of just objectifying my experiences and emotions. Once you're in a groove it's like a marriage. You get used to it, you know what to expect; you can't do anything exciting. You have to change. So I started working in prose poems. I was looking for intellectual content, I was trying to broaden my intellectual horizons, because I find that the lyric is an emotional response, whereas the prose poem is an intellectual response. The intellectual is an imaginative response. There's the difference. That is to say, in the prose poem the undercurrent is emotional, and that can be recognized in the cadences that the language takes, but the language itself is imaginative and intellectual. Whereas, in the lyric form, the language is emotive—it's an emotive kind of language, and the intellectual elements in it, are just hinted at, or are discovered in a metaphor. You have to dig it out of the metaphor. It's a difference of emphasis. I'm quite interested now in the prose poem, but from time to time I will write a straightforward lyric.

Are you conscious of being part of a movement that has grown up around the prose poem?

Very much so.

What does the prose poem do for you that a more formal poem doesn't?

The prose poem gives me so much more imaginative latitude. I'm much freer in developing the concept with which the poem first starts. Take, for example, the poem, "The Diner." The incident in "The Diner" became a kind of essay on one of the principles of existentialism—the absolute aloneness of man in the universe and how he handles it. I could've done it differently. I could've started out point-blank and said, "I'm all alone. I'm alone, and I don't know why I'm alone." I could've been very emotional about it. Instead, I preferred the wry, acceptant, logical approach. That gave me scope. What I'm looking for is imaginative scope. I can't get it if I have to concentrate on a single emotion. The lyric is emotion—right? But the prose poem is a drama; for me, it's almost like theater. Poets in this country are just exploding with prose poems. Everyone does it differently. Bly is groping for nuance. Michael Benedikt is discursive in a very charming way. I'm a poet of statement—I'm always somehow involved with the existentialist *angst*.

Do you consider yourself a romantic?

Sure. I believe in love. You can starve for lack of it. It's nothing you can order from a restaurant, so you have to

go in search of it. When you find it, you have to trans-
form yourself to hold onto it and maintain its beauty
and its value. Just as often it begins to evaporate because
it's a really spiritual quality. It's also imperative to re-
main alert, for love's disillusionment needs to keep love
either alive or find it elsewhere. That's really a romantic
tradition. That's putting love first, before physical needs
almost, or at least taking physical needs for granted, and
not love. Can't take love for granted. I think that defines
romanticism.

*Does the writing of a poem present answers for you, or
merely more questions?*

I think answers, a good many answers. My poems don't
raise any questions; all they do is state the facts, or state
the situation as is, and I take that as the reality, the solu-
tion itself. Of course, I may go back in time to write
about a subject, but it'll be from another angle—totally
different because the situation is changed for me, as for
example, a new context has developed around the whole
issue of death, and that for me creates a whole new need
for new insights. Poetry, for me, is insight.

Do you make notes for future use?

I have done it in the past, but I don't need to make notes
anymore. A poem emerges from a whole stock of mental
impressions I've had from long ago.

Are you very self-critical, or critical of others?

I'm both. I think I'm critical of myself as a poet. But it
remains for the critics to tell me if I'm critical enough.

I'm always willing to listen. I think I've done a pretty good job of keeping myself in line as a poet.

Do you find that your work makes relationships with people more difficult?

It depends. With poets, I don't have any problem. But with the average person, for example—here in this apartment house, I'm unable to reach out and invite them to my apartment for coffee and talk; I can't do that. That is the result of being a poet and writing poetry. They, I can see, are people who might be accountants or bookkeepers or garage mechanics or chauffeurs or workers in dress shops. I'll be in the elevator with them. I'll say sometimes, "How are you? Nice day. How's the weather?" and I can see they're anxious to say more, they want to say more, but they don't know how and I don't encourage it. How could you explain to them what it means to be a poet? How could you really open up to these people? How could you tell them the most important thought you've had for the day on the subject of emotion, imagination, love or life itself? They'll tell you things. They may want to tell you that they also have a deep emotional life, but they don't have the tools with which to express themselves. They can listen to you, but they become alienated from you because they're unable to meet you on verbal terms. So you find yourself talking to impassive faces. This isn't to say that they don't have those feelings. They do! But they are amazed and possibly resent your articulate abilities; you're opening up areas that they have decided they can't ever reach because it's too difficult. Maybe they even think it's too dangerous to get into that area. It might interrupt their lives. It might affect their work. It might affect their marriages. But here you are articulating. That creates a problem for them, and this is where poetry closes you off from people. That's our kind of culture. That's what technology does to people.

And that separates you. Poetry is the most powerful of the arts and because of this it has the power to make people feel stupid.

That's the great tragedy.

When you write a poem do things occur to you that were not at all in your mind when you first started the poem?

Oh yes! That's the great joy of writing a poem. Coming to a whole mine of unexplored stuff, and you just *dive* into it without a helmet and you just hope you survive all that richness that you find. It's a marvelous feeling, digging out a few shovelfuls of that stuff. That's what I look for in a poem, a new adventure, a new depth.

Have you ever described a situation of which you have no personal experience other than a believability in the poem itself?

Oh yes. All three ritual poems I've never actually experienced. It's an art to make a poem as convincing as reality.

Do you ever go through periods where you don't work at all? Where you find you can't write?

That's happened. I've stopped writing because I haven't

been able to resolve my personal life, where I couldn't face certain events in my life and didn't want to write about them falsely.

What do you do then?

I keep in touch with people by correspondence. I do a lot of editing. I make phone calls. I worry about money. I see people. I go to the theater. I keep in touch with friends. I keep busy. I wash the floors. I do my laundry. Work on my school work.

Have you ever written about not being able to write?

That's what I'm doing in my journals.

What about in your poetry?

I've done that too! But it doesn't solve the problem. It doesn't stimulate a solution to the inner conflicts.

How real to you are your poems after the poems are finished?

Oddly enough, it takes quite a few years to recognize their reality. For example, the poems I wrote in the 1950s, when I was writing them, they weren't the reality; the reality was the living itself. At the time I thought that this was just filling in a couple of hours with release— relief from torture, or relief from life. But now I see they *are* the life.

Can you think of any one of your poems in your experience that in its reading has led you to a mood of despair?

Yes, some of the poems about my son. I sometimes break down when I read them.

Which poem are you most proud of?

"Rescue the Dead."

Do you have a stance in either confronting your own poetry as you write it or looking at somebody else's?

For myself, I try to take the most truthful position toward the poem in relation to the experience. In relation to other poets, I *try* to remain as catholic in my view as I can. I really will work very hard, where the poem is difficult, to become involved with it and see it from the inside.

Do you have a sense of limitation?

Definitely. I don't think I could live without a sense of limitation. Sometimes you feel that you're unlimited, but it's very scary. When you're writing a poem that's very exciting. It's so intense you think you're leaving yourself. That's important to the experience. In fact, it's invaluable. Then you know how close you get to death. What's limitless is death, life is limited. It's good to get back to life—after you've written a poem.

I sometimes get the impression that you find writing poems a burden. That you become restless, that this sense of restlessness can be felt in the poem.

Sometimes writing a poem *is* a burden. It doesn't always answer the problems. When you aren't particularly interested in writing, but you have no other choice but to write—that's happened often. It's like being imprisoned, and you have no choice but to do what's limited to the life of the prison. And the writing is hard to do—very hard.

Are there any poems of a kind that you haven't written before that you visualize yourself writing?

Sure! I'd like to write great poetic drama! A tremendous epic! I'd like to write great epics. I'd like to write the last poem of the world.

That's an interesting concept!

I tried that in one little poem. Shall I read it to you? This poem has no title to it, and I thought of it as the last poem of the world.

> I am dreaming of the funeral of the world, watching it go by carried in an urn, reduced to ashes, and followed by a horde of mourners, a million abreast, across the broadest lands and all chanting together, We are dead, we have killed ourselves. We are beyond rescue. What you see is not us but your thoughts of us, and I who am observing in terror of it being true hope not to have to wake up, so that I may let myself discount it as a dream.

It's great! It works on two levels at once: it works on the level of the waking world and on the level of the sleeping world.

Well, I hope it's not the last poem in the world.

It's a prose poem, isn't it?

Can you tell it's a prose poem? How?

By the way you read it; by the way my ear is receiving it.

You may be right. I can't judge those things.

Cocteau said, "Know what you can do well and don't do it." Would you say that the kind of poem you write or perhaps the prose poem is something you do well, and, with this in mind, have you ever considered changing to another kind of writing?

I have to do something that I can't define for myself now. Maybe it's a return to the direct, very personal lyric. I've been writing a lot of love poems. They are very personal, very direct and open—explicit. I'm more comfortable with that right now. The emotion dominates the poem rather than the concept.

Your sensibilities have changed?

I'm wandering—I'm going in circles.

Who have you been reading lately?

I picked up Shakespeare recently. I became really excited. I see him more clearly now than ever before. His language really is thrilling—it's virtually always on target. He's very much part of the present. I went through John Donne lately, too, and I was very much delighted. He's a great wit. I was overjoyed that such a man has been around for so many years. I tried some of Hopkins but couldn't take too much of him.

You're so widely read now, among poets and students alike, and studied, in fact, on many campuses, that one rarely meets anybody interested in contemporary

American poetry who doesn't at least know your name. In fact, you've eclipsed a great many poets you had to deal with back in the 1940s. How do you account for this?

Well, I guess my style anticipated the style and the sensibility that today is prevalent among the young and maybe among college teachers. I started out with a sense of doom and frustration. I guess we've reached that point in our history. My personal frustration—my personal sense of tragedy has become the metaphor for the sense of tragedy we feel nationally.

Do you account for becoming generally known among a younger generation of poets because they did not try to write like the generation to which you properly belong by age—a generation of let's say Lowell, Berryman, Schwartz?

Seeing it from the point of view of the students, well, then, the answer would be yes. They wouldn't want to write like Lowell or Berryman. Neither of them took their lives seriously enough or saw their lives in its tragic context. There's a sense of distaste in Lowell's work, a kind of disdain for his life—a weariness with it. Berryman has a kind of contempt, too—for himself.

They're kind of snobby.

They found themselves in this menial society. They, of superior craft, of superior mentality and education and social status, having to deal with these problems of everyday living, which, according to their education and background, should have been of very little consequence to them. They couldn't escape it. So they have a contempt for their material. I had a struggle with my demons, and I took them very seriously and that was the difference.

What is the recurring metaphor of walking *that you employ in your work? What does it mean to you?*

Well, *walking* to me is *thinking*—going from one object to another, a way of working things out.

What do dreams mean to you and how do you apply them to your writing? I'm thinking of such poems as "The Errand Boy" or the poem entitled "The Dream," which is in Say Pardon.

They're flashes of insight that penetrate the banalities and clichés of everyday life. I know that something is going on beneath the surface that's really the life we're living, *not* that surface cliché. So I discovered a good mode of expression is through bizarre arrangements of images we call dreams.

Do you write the dream out as it actually happened, sequence by sequence?

I invent the dream.

Do you record dreams?

Actually I don't. Virtually every poem in the book *Facing the Tree*—every dream poem is an invented dream. These are metaphors for states of mind which are below the surface of my everyday conversation. I invent them in order to have access to the insights below the surface.

This is how I state these insights. I can't find any other way—I have to imagine.

What is it that you find in Vallejo or Williams, besides their ability to be totally open in confronting the world, that's so dynamic?

The language of the guts. The hard language of living; the language of hard living, the universal language.

Which is what? By way of the heart to the mind?

By way of the muscles. The muscles have to react to living. It's rare to find that muscularity in poetry, in the lines of the poets where you can feel the mind running like an electric current through the muscles.

What is important to you?

The most important thing is peace of mind—growing out of an assurance about one's relationships with others. Relationships that you can count on that won't backfire—on which you can turn your back and not fear some sort of a reprisal or betrayal. It's a dependence thing. You have a relationship which becomes a metaphor for your relationships with the rest of the world. If it's a secure and loving relationship on which you can count for your needs, physical, mental, and emotional, then you have what most people lack. You have going for yourself a balanced energizing situation. Then you can turn around and put your energy into a lot of different things because you can take this other thing for granted. A person loves you. You know that this love will not fail you under virtually any circumstance. This love is for you and you alone. Something for you which is for no one else. That's important. When you have that I think you have a treasure.

What are you working on at the moment aside from the love poems?

Well, I'm thinking about how everything is related to everything else. It's a world of oneness really which has been hidden from us by the world of specialization into which we are plunged. The world of technocracy makes too prominent and too important such utilities as the refrigerator, or the car, and a special kind of car, to separate it from all other cars. You can say this all comes from the earth. Everything is from the earth. We're from the earth. We're all intimately involved with one another and with each other. We're intimately related. You can only distinguish yourself by maybe your name, because you might find a mirror image of yourself in some other person and it would amaze you, but it happens. I'm not saying that that mirror image would be writing the same kind of poetry you write. That's not it. But you see responses that are strikingly similar to yours in situations. It raises a lot of questions. The body is attracted to other bodies. All bodies are attracted to one another, really. What then is love? We all love one another. Beneath the surface of race, conflict, social conflict, money conflict, nation conflict, we're all very much alike and we could love one another, at least in the abstract. We know, theoretically—we've seen it happen. An American soldier falls in love with a Vietnamese girl because bodies are all informed with the same need to have other bodies. So when we see all is one then why do we take one for all? Interesting question. Why do we take one for all? Well, could it be that we will it so? Is this a cultural phenomenon? These are questions I ask myself. If all is one why do we choose one for all? I ask myself *is this necessary?* You know this whole concept of romanticizing a relationship. The whole concept of love. Not every society believes in it. They really encourage it in this society and it causes terrible trouble—an awful mess. And I'm the worst offender of all [both burst out laughing]. The Chinese are perfectly realistic. They marry their children to one another before the child is even aware. They recognize that the whole idea of love is an illusion, because it's love for everyone. You have to love everyone—anyone and everyone.

If you had to describe how you're feeling now in your life and work in a few words, how would you do it?

Well, I'm drifting, ecstatic at times; sad at times—drifting, I seem to be caught in some kind of a rapids and I don't know where it's taking me. I'm terribly excited about it, because I willed it so.

Well, maybe willing certain situations, but never knowing what the outcome will be, because the outcome becomes the beginning of something else.

That's right. I don't know the outcome because my will is in suspension at the moment. So, I'm ecstatic at times and very sad at times.

Or your will or your love is in suspension. What book of yours would you consider your most decisive? Decisive in the sense that the poetry in it was the most original and the most astonishing for you?

I'd say *Rescue the Dead* at the moment.

I would say Facing the Tree *is the most original and the most astonishing. Great leaps and bounds.*

I simply haven't absorbed it yet.

How do you feel about your Selected Poems *and the* Notebooks *looking back at them?*

The *Notebooks* I wish I'd been able to expand much more. A lot of material had to be left out. I think we got the essence of it; the spiritual essence is fairly clear. As for the *Selected,* well, there isn't anything I can say for or against it. It's just an object. When you've published your selected poems people are astonished when the next book comes out; they think this guy is dead! Well, the old man is dead, the old poet is dead. The new one is on his way.

Do you see yourself in some way being or becoming a major influence on American poetry? Have poets come around to your way of thinking?

I think most poets have caught up with me now. So I think what I really am in is a kind of a tradition—carrying out a tradition, rather than hacking out a new wilderness. From that point of view, it's rather unfortunate if I find poets copying me in any way. I feel that they're falling behind.

What do you think of Allen Ginsberg?

Ginsberg's influence was tremendously overpowering for awhile. I think he is suffering from a decline of his influence—if it's of any importance to him. His influence no longer shows itself. By that I mean, the poets who felt him strongly aren't around to give his work that kind of an ambience; that radiance, that intensity it once had. Instead, they've taken his surface changes, his surface appearances. His best work remains very powerful. But, believe it or not—believe this or not!—the young poets I'm in touch with now think that he's almost totally irrelevant for the 1970s. They can see that "Kaddish" is a nice poem, a moving poem, but it doesn't affect them. "Howl" doesn't even apply to them. They're not in that kind of a groove. That applies to my work, too. I don't feel myself any longer unaccepted, left out, exiled. That does something. Except with certain critics, like Harold Bloom, or poets and critics like Richard Howard who have pretensions to the genteel tradition on a plane of abstraction within transcendentalism, or A. R. Ammons elected to carry on this tradition within transcendentalism. If that became the dominant sensibility in this country again, I would have a fight on my hands again. My own sensibility would once more become radicalized in confrontation with genteelism. But that has become peripheral to contemporary poetry. Writers like Harold Bloom and Richard Howard are peripheral to American poetry. They never were at the center either, except Ammons who still could be, but apparently under the influence of Harold Bloom has spread himself very thin. I'm one of a group which is at the center, the living center of contemporary poetry today. That doesn't make me stand out any longer as a major influence. There isn't any poet standing head and shoulders above others today, in that sense. Maybe we're all trying to find a way to emerge from the web in which we are living. Where is the new frontier? For me, it can only be very personal. Whether it has a significance eventually in poetry, I couldn't estimate at this time. I know that I personally am confronting new frontiers, and it's scaring the shit out of me. It's like being in space. It's tremendously exhilarating, too. I'm going to have to make certain sacrifices. But that's all personal. That's of no significance at the moment in poetry.

You've stated in the Boundary 2 *interview that "more than ever I'm convinced that political poetry is here to stay." What is your own sense of the poet as political writer?*

Politics, to me means *how to run a government.* Since we have a social structure that needs someone to govern it, there are values involved. To me political poetry is not a matter of getting on a platform—denouncing or pronouncing your values, the way you feel the values are failing among individuals, or among nations or within a particular government. Yet the technique by which we can avoid writing a kind of political poem that sounds like an agitprop *is* to do it through the person. The poet should do it through his own sensibility and not through a whole series of ideological statements. That to me is ridiculous. I saw that sort of thing being done by the Communist party in the 1930s and I rejected it immediately. Not only was it impersonal, but it was dehumanizing—the sort of thing they were asking poets to do. I decided I had to give up that method, but I couldn't give up the principle of arguing the *large* issues. The large issues of life and death as related to the conduct of a state, how to conduct a social system. The individual poet must respond to political issues from his own experiences and from reading and from a general sense of what is right and wrong. It can never be ideological.

In light of what we've been discussing in regards to poetry and criticism, Robert Bly has stated in one of his columns in APR, *that "we can let the academic imagina-*

tion regain the control over American poetry that it had during the time of the New Critics or we can fight." Do you think that this regaining of control Bly talks about is in reference to the fact that now that Williams and Olson are dead their sphere of influence on younger poets is no longer a threat to the genteel or academically oriented poets and critics, and that one way that we can overcome their regaining control is to follow Lincoln's example of the warrior energy by forcing the issue to band together, to fight them in print where it hurts? I remember reading somewhere that Lincoln said, "To sin by silence when they should protest makes cowards of men."

Well, I think that would be a somewhat perverse statement made by Bly, perhaps meant to be ironical. It doesn't sound like Bly, you know. I think Bly was simply stating the alternatives, otherwise it sounds like what the Communists used to say at the time before Hitler came into power, "We've got to let Hitler come into power so we can have something to fight for." It's idiotic because the catastrophe was enormous. No, I hardly believe Bly meant that. No. In fact, I think that our view of the influence of Williams and Olson today as declining is not quite correct. The influence is still very great—still remains at its crest, as far as I can see from the poems I'm getting at the *American Poetry Review* and other places. The use of the free form remains paramount among all poets that I know of, established poets and learning poets. So, I don't see what the issue is here.

Has a new kind of academia arisen lately?

Yes. Men like Bloom, for example, and John Hollander who writes in free form, but whose poetic sensibility is overly refined and recherché. You don't get the harsh impact that Williams searched for and which Olson also presented. What I mean when I say harsh impact, is the kind of life both of them had to live which was the only kind of life they had. They had no choices, you see. Neither of them was an academic and neither thought of making his living in college or by writing in such a way as to appeal to a genteel tradition. That wasn't what interested them. They had their backs to the genteel audience and their faces toward the life around them which they were participating in. What's happened is that the powerful influence of men like Williams and Olson has gone very deeply into the writings of the genteel tradition, so that the academics have had to absorb their techniques and with these techniques are once more asserting a kind of quietism, an intellectualism that both Williams and Olson would have totally rejected.

Because it wasn't enough?

It's not rounded enough.

Or not enough of a commitment.

That's right. I'm thinking of John Ashbery, for example, though he reaches passages of acute evocatory insights.

Do you still sense a critical resistance to your work? Why and where is it coming from?

I think it comes from the genteel tradition. They certainly sense that I'm opposed to contemplative poetry in the sense of withdrawal from life. I'm very pleased that there *are* a number of critics who side with me and work toward making my poems better known, but there is still a very strong resistance from men like Bloom and Hollander and Richard Howard. They have a strong resistance because I threaten their basic assumption about poetry which is that language takes precedence over content. They think through language you learn of life. I say you learn of life through sensibility which then has to be translated into language. Their tradition is a bastard romanticism. If you look carefully at the romantic tradition you'll see that it began with sensibility—resistance to the intellectualization of poetry in the eighteenth century. Wordsworth resisted it by personalizing his poetry with the language he was born into and raised with. So the fight is still there. It's a kind of seesaw fight. Right now I would say that the prestigious prizes on the whole are going to those favored by the genteel tradition.

Did you find yourself, after Williams's death, suddenly alone again?

No, I didn't. I had some marvelous friendships among poets: Jim Wright, Robert Bly, Stanley Kunitz, William Meredith, Harvey Shapiro, Armand Schwerner, Jerome Mazzaro, Ralph J. Mills, Jr. They've been very good to me.

But at the time of Williams's death did you go through the struggle of lack of optimism of some kind of support?

Well, I felt that it meant the beginning of the kind of regression we've been talking about: the reassertion of the genteel tradition. It had more or less gone into the background. His influence had gained tremendously just before his death. The young were flocking to him, learning from him in every way. Well, with his death I felt we had lost a powerful, exciting force in the midst of the enemy, the elite.

It's as if he had handed you the torch.

That was the feeling I had. Not only me, but he gave it to a few of us.

But I think the others were well on their way already. Olson already had his school of poetry behind him—was plunging on.

Well, I still felt myself alone in the sense that I didn't actually have followers, not that I wanted any; but, you know, it inevitably happens when a poet publishes a large body of work he draws the attention of other poets who are beginners who will tend to model themselves on his work. I find that makes me very uncomfortable. Your own work returns to you through the psyche of another poet and he or she is not doing it quite the way you would want it to be done. It's not right. I get poems dedicated to me from poets and some of them really send me up the wall. With the years I came to realize that I had a lot of friends all the while and they stepped forward or I reached out to them, too.

I like what you just said about reaching out to them because you bring across a certain kind of a generosity from a part of your personality that comes across in your work as well as in other areas.

I always seem to find where the water is coming from.

1979

III

Essays, Lectures, Reviews

Introduction to *William Carlos Williams*
A Memorial Chapbook

This chapbook of poems by foreign and American poets was conceived during Williams's last year among us, with no thought of his approaching death. Many of us were aware of the seriousness of his illness which had deprived him of the use of his right arm. His speech had been severely impaired. He was in a depressed mood and had virtually given up any attempt to continue writing, but so strong was the influence of Williams, the doer, that we received the news of our eyes and ears through the pulsation of his lines. We saw and heard him fighting, buoyant, unshaken, and undefeated. It was the occasion for a chapbook of poems in joyful hailing of the man and his life.

It was at my last visit to his house several months before his death that I sensed Williams was going rapidly. His depression had turned into a kind of triumphant bitterness in which he looked forward to death as an event. He yearned for it and spoke as if it were something lacking in his work that he needed to round out his poetry and thought. Coincidentally, poems had begun to arrive for the chapbook somber and foretelling of death. None directly presaged his own, yet they were dark with such a sense of it that I could not hesitate to accept them, especially now that his situation had indeed become grave. These tragic poems were added to the chapbook. They are there to take note of his death with all the power that is in them, while the collection ends with poems of continuing love, pleasure, and enthusiasm, as Williams would have approved.

At this high moment of his fame, it is almost superfluous to enumerate the man's qualities as poet, they are so well-known, loved, and appreciated. He stands beside Walt Whitman, a world figure, with *Paterson,* a poem of tragic and universal import. Its theme is at the root of every social and political upheaval in the world today. In *Paterson,* Williams delineates this theme as the failure of language, the failure of communication, of necessity referring to himself as poet and contemporary in the grip of this modern dilemma, but this is only to point at the basic failure among men themselves in their attitude toward one another and toward life. It is one of separation. "Divorce is the sign of knowledge in our times," from which springs those calamities that we now witness among men, women and nations. Williams takes the small, nearly obscure city of Paterson as his focal point, weaving symbol and reality around it on each level of society, using himself as the operational figure, sometimes as the city itself, often as man, as woman, and as the great, roaring, dumb Passaic waterfalls pouring down from above the city its torrent of power without direction, except as dying in the sea, without purpose, without soul, which is to say, without language. Like *Leaves of Grass,* it is a work unprecedented in scope and intent in American literature, and as with *Leaves of Grass* comes of harsh reality in collision with an exuberant and loving man. A poem of such courageous insight and resolution was hardly to be expected in these despairing times, but then it was like Williams to go counter to the prevailing current, to state life's fullest potential against the force of the fashionable. *Paterson* is read with intense interest here and abroad. It has restored among men our first truth and idealism. In Williams America lives and is honored.

1963

Williams's Influence

Some Social Aspects

A study of the vital role played by William Carlos Williams in the work of American poets would actually be a review of the accomplishments of the important poets today. I say this in awareness of the once nearly universal influence of Eliot and the New Criticism as enunciated by Ransom, Tate, Blackmur, and others. Williams has awakened voices that have never before been heard in our literature. I am referring here to a whole stratum, or substratum, to be precise, of our society that until recently remained hidden away in its own misery and shame. Today it may well be that theirs is the pervasive voice in American poetry, with Allen Ginsberg as their chief spokesman. Add to this the fact of unparalleled high-level activity among the academically situated poets, most of whom are writing verse utterly changed from the metaphysical canon taught at Kenyon College and in Eliot's lectures. Further, there are those who cannot be classified with any particular group or tendency, yet have felt the impact of Williams's ideas. They can be counted by the score from a simple examination of the pages of the small literary magazines.

Considering the extent and depth of this influence, virtually supplanting that of Eliot and his school, it can be looked on as a major social phenomenon. Primarily, it is in reaction to the two chief, indivisible positions held by Eliot plus certain members of the New Criticism: their clericalism and their detachment from the social scene. By their own acknowledgment they have taught a studied withdrawal from society, in which is implicit a condemnation of the present state of our culture. Williams, by contrast (see *Paterson,* his masterwork), stands at exact center, encouraging people to accept themselves. Without confidence and trust in themselves, he contends, nothing can be accomplished for the general good or, by extension, for the life of poetry: the country's spirit. Without respect for one's own identity, the person is lost.

Historically, the earliest and most important poet to come directly in contact with Williams's teaching was Louis Zukofsky, himself the founder of the objectivist school. Zukofsky, like Pound, through whom he met Williams, was a scholar-poet from the start, with much of the impatience of Pound and even more acerbity. Banality and loose thinking in American poetry were the two cardinal sins which Zukofsky fought from the outset of his career. To him, they reflected the softness and vacuity, the general unreality in American life itself at that time. In 1948, he published *A Test of Poetry,* a manual of poetic taste that has become required reading for all who would write well and seriously. But already another and even more important facet of Zukofsky came to light through his personal friendship with Williams. Zukofsky had been writing a kind of verse which sought to eliminate so-called extraneous, obtrusive elements, particularly rhetoric and transitional matter: two of the main weaknesses in American poetry. Through the image Zukofsky sought to eliminate these faults.

A highly formal verse emerged, as a result, which tended to limit the flow of ideas and feelings. Nuance, sublety, thought, modifications, were difficult if not impossible to convey in this static picture poetry. Imagination was threatened, at the price of avoiding sentimentality, and feelings put under grim lock. American poets and their audiences were uneasy with this. While certain features of objectivism remained valid for Zukofsky, such as strictly economical line and a pinpointing by image of emotion or idea, his appreciation of Williams's humanist art awoke him to the dangers implicit in his method.

In summary, it can be said that where Williams is satisfied with setting down his ideas in concrete terms of the present, Zukofsky goes on to find the hidden relationships with historical ideas and situations. He has made of his own work a branch of an ancient humanism, Greek in origin, and has created a sense of continuity and tradition for the moderns. Consequently, he has evolved a perspective that has helped gain for Williams's work the respect and admiration it now enjoys. Williams's boldness was fortified by Zukofsky's careful ruminations on the past.

Like Zukofsky in temperament, but of a later generation and condition, is Charles Olson. While they diverge on important points, a meeting between them would yield very amiable conversation, with much sympathy for each other's views. Like Zukofsky, Olson has been a scholar-poet from the start. However, he has been after a kind of communication which if carried to its logical climax, as in his *Maximus* poems, would eliminate the human factor which makes Zukofsky's work strong. In his famous *Theory of Field Composition,* Olson develops his ideas at length. While essentially they derive from Williams's earlier theory of variable open form, Olson's emphasis is on perception, especially as grasped by the intellect. Coming at a time when deep dissatisfaction with the elaborate closed stanzaic forms had already begun to develop, the *Theory,* published in 1950, had an electrifying effect on college students of poetry. Olson contended, in opposition to the teaching of metaphysical poetry, that the intellect should be directed primarily toward perceptions other than one's own mental and emotional behavior. The mind, he argues, must be made to study and record data of the objective world, if only for its own enrichment and stimulation. The mind actually could build a poetry from the sheer ordering of these perceptions within the scope it sets itself. To these young poets looking inward according to the metaphysical formula, the *Theory* came as an illumination in the dark of their skulls. In the era of the Eisenhower euphoria, when people appeared content and well-fed, poets wondered whether this state of mind was suited to introspective metaphysical poetry. In the light of this skepticism, Olson's position offered these poets an escape and a unique opportunity to look outward.

Thus Olson's contribution to an appreciation and furtherance of Williams's ideas and practices among American poets was perhaps of pivotal importance, since interest in poetry resides mainly in colleges today, from which it then spreads outwards. In his own poetry, the accruing *Maximus* poems represent a major effort to restate once more the integrity of the person as an individual in the objective world, with the special implications, however, of New England history and the Puritan conscience.

One of the effects of Olson's teaching, and the publication of his seminal poem, *The Kingfishers,* as if in support of his *Theory,* was a decisive split from the Eliot-Ransom-Tate camp. Poets who had already published their first volumes in the accepted interior cerebral style began a cautious experimentation with a variable measure built around sensed things. James Wright, Robert

Bly, W. S. Merwin, and Donald Hall came to be noticed for the changes taking place in their styles, and lately have begun to exhibit consummate work in their new personal commitments. Today as college teachers and/or editors and poets, they are bringing student poets along with them into direct involvement in the American scene. The Olson penumbra remains, but this new trend now serves to alleviate the mental astringency of the Black Mountain (Olson) school, in favor of "projecting" rather than "perceiving" life. Of this new group, it can be said that it offers the best hope to date of a bridge between two opposing sensibilities in our country.

Of the poets involved in Williams's influence, Denise Levertov is closest to his tenets, as to the balance of elements that go into a poem. Her mind is never in conflict with its perceived objects or attendant reactions. She seems limited only by the limitations of her experience. Tolerance and a sense of forward movement are principal qualities in her writing. This accords with Williams's doctrine that a poet to advance in his poetry must simultaneously advance into the life of his or her times. Denise Levertov's work suggests a chance of pulling together the many contending poetic forces under the Williams banner and giving them the unifying national style that is still lacking. Hers is the voice of belief in self, subscribing to Williams's prescription for the health of our country and its achievements.

Last, the loudest and perhaps most telling at this time among the schools is that led by Allen Ginsberg. In view of what has developed from and within him, it is ironic to note that he considers himself a disciple of Williams. Ginsberg launched a movement that may yet be recognized as the temper of our times, as did Eliot in his day. Logically enough, Ginsberg's relation to Eliot has not been overlooked either by his admirers, or critics. There is in these two poets, otherwise so oddly paired, the same sense of spiritual disaster and need for salvation. In Eliot, of course, the expression is in intellectual terms. Ginsberg speaks for a whole section of beleaguered, dispossessed, and obscure people who have known neither self-respect nor decent, tangible sympathy from others. These are the vast substrata in our society imprisoned by poverty, illness, and ignorance. He speaks with their bitter self-hatred and world-hatred, all that is left for them as positive values to count on in their lives. At the same time he cries with their hallucinatory voice for what will never be, but what they will never cease yearning for, a life of inner beauty and transcendency. All this is said in the words and within the context of their available experience. It is not a walk in Eliot's garden, but a walk through littered streets after a drug injection that will sweep away the filth at their feet and set them on a cloud closer to an invisible, unspeaking God. These are facts out of Ginsberg's own existence, shared with the alienated, and the poetry that has come out of this life has gone around the world as the most striking and prevalent image of our land.

Following publication of *Howl* a torrent of poetry was loosed from all sides. The best and most representative of this new wave was brought together in *The New American Poetry 1945-1960* (Grove Press) edited by Donald M. Allen. Many of the contributors refer explicitly to prison, reformatories, asylums, drugs, and sexual deviation in their poems and biographical sketches. Just as Eliot had questioned and undermined the accepted mores and assumed progressiveness of his day, these poets who had declared themselves liberated by Williams as individuals set about rejecting and tearing to pieces the very fabric with which Williams had validated his poems. The individual in whom the strength of Williams's poetry and ideas should reside is shown so tormented, beaten, imprisoned, drugged, raped, maddened, that if anything of the person is left, it is the hysterical need to recite his destruction. The beats, to the world abroad, intellectuals and artists generally, represent the most powerful current in American poetry today. The strong division of feeling among American writers themselves about the beats occurs, as might be expected, very nearly along social lines, the academicians and the sophisticated, college-trained Olsonites strongly in opposition. But for all the repugnance with which Ginsberg's themes and style have been generally treated, the effect of his productions, including his recent *Kaddish,* has been to bring about a new sense of adventure even among these same academicians, though within their own spheres. Sex, social deviation, personal complications are handled far more freely and openly than in the past. Despite the blow Ginsberg and his followers unwittingly dealt the Williams ethos of the integrated individual, and perhaps in reaction, which would be typical of American poets, the result has been a reassertion of the person. The fact remains that the liveliest work today, distinguished by a strong personal vision in free, open, variable patterns, includes the work of the beats at their best.

Among those who do not fit readily into any category, I would mention these outstanding poets: Robert Lowell, Robert Duncan, Theodore Roethke, Randall Jarrell, Kenneth Rexroth, and Byron Vazakas, to name a few. All are marked by a very pronounced sense of independence and self. It is clear that they are governed in keeping with Williams's dictum, by the esthetic of personal confrontation with their subject. There are others, far too many to name here, whom I deeply value for their struggle to react to their objective situation with the full measure and art of their beings. It is these poets, outside any school, who add such a rich cross-coloration to the entire poetic scene and who by their very independence and vitality are the pride of American culture.

Now, an essential of Williams's teaching has been that the poet must commit himself to his country. This all poets have followed faithfully each in his fashion, but a paradox, perhaps foreseen by Williams himself in his despairing moods, has been the indifference of the country itself to these intensely national poets. There have been intermittent instances of appreciation, such as a presidential invitation to Robert Frost for the inaugural; and there are inconsistent efforts of funds and foundations to encourage poets by subsidies that often fall to those whose reputations are already established or who have arrived financially through their own efforts in other fields. A certain aura of timidity hangs over these foundations that fear to offend conventional public taste which, as every poet and critic knows, must be led and taught—Ezra Pound's first and truest dictum, as valid today as then. But poets still must serve as one another's mentors and judges in a kind of inbred isolation.

Even more cogently, in Williams's belief, the individual must make his way into the life of society if he would write meaningfully at all and gain stature. He has no other choice in a country so constituted that a man finds himself at the very heart of the social structure, is himself society. In such an open society, he cannot lose himself in class identification but must grow as a person in his own right, carrying with him all the seeds of his actions for good and bad. This is both a stimulating and agonizing situation for the poet as man and citizen. At the same time, in the role of poet, he owes something to the image of his country and must profess an identity with it. In view of the negligence with which his country treats him, this is an irony almost too heavy to bear.

Yet poets do live and write. They work at trades, professions, or simply at taking handouts, as sometimes in the case of the beats. The more sophisticated and college-trained poets eke out a living on protracted fellowships, short periods working at the few colonies, and sadly limited returns from magazines and books. Today many poems express futility, a sense of desolation, a mood of day-to-day survival. What a distance from Williams's now classic world of *Paterson*. There, hope never fell so low that the hustle and bustle of life itself did not stimulate the poet out of his despair. It was a world where you could count on seeing the next day, and the next, and the next. Today most of the poets in the wake of Williams live and work in megapolitan centers where life has none of the daily charm he found in outlying Paterson or Rutherford. In the vast, formless, and sprawling aggregations such as New York and Chicago, poets derive their sense of life from each day's precarious experiences. They have yet to find ways to love their lives with the zest and freedom which Williams brought to his. In great part, this painful difference explains the appeal of Allen Ginsberg and his adherents. The threat from the sky, the threat of muggings and knifings just around the corner, the demoralization of a despised, meaningless work routine—among the main characteristics of city life—inform the milieu in which Ginsberg chants his hallucinatory songs of sex and drugs, escape exits and no exits. Where once a man felt able to order his own destiny and the country to direct itself, as in Williams's vision, the feeling is that this liberty has been taken out of one's hands. But the man and the poet mean to live, and to speak of that too in poems, personal poems. The Williams creed founded on the strength and independence of the individual continues to assert, through paradox and rejection, the only important values: the sanctity of life, of the person, of the being in continual process, which shall have poems to say it.

1964

Remembering Williams

One night, after giving a reading from his poems, Williams joined me in the street on the way to a bar and as we walked in silence for a while (I was just too shy to start a conversation with this vigorous, outspoken man) he suddenly burst out to say—I wish I could recall his exact words—"There is no competition among poets!" Was it something that he had detected in me, reading it in my silence? Was I in competition with the great, clarion Williams? Was he speaking to me directly? These are questions in hindsight. I can't recall having felt as he may have sensed in me. I felt rather that he was addressing himself to the poets who were among his audience and who had remained silent after his having abruptly, with only the briefest introduction, interrupted his reading to read from a poem of mine to illustrate his principles of composition. He had just reviewed my first book of poems for the *New York Times* and apparently was still involved with it mentally. They, the audience, with distinguished American poets seated there, remained silent. I was stunned by Williams's sudden decision to read from my poems and was equally stunned by the

This piece serves as an introduction to a catalogue of Williams materials from the Baumgardner Collection at Kent State.

175

silence he had met. If during our short walk to the bar he was thinking about that silence (the review had appeared in the Sunday book section only two days earlier) then I could understand his outburst. In his vigorous manner, the words yet sounded plaintive, the sound of a visionary disappointed in the company of poets. I was moved and unhappy at his unhappiness, and what did I say to try to console him or was it to support him in his anger of which disappointment was the root? Again I can't recall exactly because I was too awed by the presence of the man himself, but how I have since acted in my relationship to most poets may be an indication of what I actually did say then and felt moved to say. I recall agreeing with him emphatically. I could not see myself competing with Williams. I could not see myself competing with any poets, for that matter. How could such a behavior be reconciled with the writing of poetry out of one's deepest, most sensitive self, that which was nourished and lived by a pleasure in living? Was this not Williams's whole meaning? It was what I had gathered from his poems, and it had drawn me out of my abstract touchiness toward life, and so to take pleasure in one's life meant too to take pleasure in the lives of others who, logically, were enjoying their lives. There could be no competition among men and women, certainly not among poets, in that circumstance, and I could see in this the basis for Williams's plaintive remark. Women and men, poets in particular, could and should want to act together to sustain and further a life of pleasure in themselves and in others. In brief, to cooperate and collaborate in keeping such a way of life ever strong and fresh. Well, that was the ideal apparently which for all of Williams's openness to living had failed for him that evening, but it was a lesson in generosity and selfless dedication I was never to forget and that, as I look back, in particular on his letters to me, most of which are lodged in this library [Kent State University Library], I find so marvelously illustrated there.

But if these letters to me had been unique for Williams, it would have been a contradiction in spirit for him. I sensed, as I first received them, that he was writing out of a passionate dialogue with others long before I had come on the scene. I read them on two levels, the first, naturally, as addressed to me. (How could I have imagined such an outpouring from this most daring of American poets in response to my first book?) The second level was that of his critical theories that virtually raged through the letters, as if he was addressing others beyond me, and it was truly so, as I could read in the significant small phrases that stood out here and there that indicated a powerful, ongoing debate with another world, strange to me then, the world of literary dogma. It certainly was not my world, far removed by work and circumstance, from the world of abstract opinion on writing, and I could sense further from this that Williams was in need of and in constant search of an audience that could listen and absorb what he had to say, in contrast to the silence he was meeting in the literary world, that in singling me out for this excited, intellectual discussion, he had found another potential adherent or at least another ear and eye that would listen and/or read him with attention. I was but one among many, many, as eventually I found confirmed in the dozens of letters he was to write to new and young poets in whose work he could discover his theories and practice being successfully realized. And so I count myself among those many and fortunate, very fortunate for that at a critical period in my life. There's no doubt in my mind that the material the reader will find in this catalogue will bear out my sense of a man and poet highly charged with a mission to transform the world of literature, poetry especially, into the vision that was inspiring him in his own poems, that of openness to experience, to change, to significant order, to adventurous thought and feeling, to language that could communicate in every shade of subtlety, evoking life in every shade—the language of everyday discourse on every level of society. This was the only language that could fulfill such a demanding task, and Williams succeeded in his own work. We can see his success in virtually all contemporary American poets since his death, paradoxically even among our surrealist poets. Williams will stand forever as the man, after Whitman, who, in his time, liberated the language from its specious metaphysical cast and who brought to literature a community of purpose to this end: that life be lived to its fullest and written of with that power of fullness.

1978

The Necessity of the Personal

"Forget all rules, forget all restrictions, as to taste, as to what ought to be said," wrote William Carlos Williams in an article, "How to Write," published in 1936.

> Write for the pleasure of it—whether slowly or fast—every form of resistance to a complete release should be abandoned. For today we know the meaning of depth, it is a primitive profundity of the personality that must be touched if what we do is to have it. The faculties untied, proceed backward through the night of our unconscious past. It goes down to the ritualistic, amoral past of the race, to fetish, to dream, to wherever the "genius" of the particular writer finds itself able to go.

Whether Williams's statement is or is not the direct cause, the proliferation of personal styles in American poetry today is unprecedented in scope and variety. It is virtually impossible to give a complete description without overlooking something new gestating in obscurity at that moment. Clearly, Williams's dictum, together with the more revolutionary impulse of that day, has had its effect upon the vast majority of American poets. In this talk, I shall limit my description to certain outstanding developments, without prejudice toward those others of equal importance that must be omitted for lack of space, or more to the point, because to describe them would actually parallel, at least in principle, those already described. At any rate, the theme of this talk, while it arises from this extraordinary diversity, is in my effort to go beyond that for an understanding of its significance for poetry as a whole.

To make a point by contrast, I begin with a discussion of the classical or traditional as practiced today. It has the grudging respect of the nonconformists for the stubbornness with which it is pursued by a small but steady island of poets, each of undoubted integrity in his or her chosen traditional mode. About that, it may even be said that it has served as a useful reference point of departure for others in the school of Williams and beyond. Of those continuing to identify with the classical forms and meters, I would name Anthony Hecht and Richard Wilbur among the most skillful and original. Their originality stems precisely from their adaptation of contemporary themes and tones to the demands of their particular imposed forms. I think it is a brave attempt to bridge an unbridgeable gulf. In their poems, the modern sensibility of horror, anger, and divisiveness has been given the formal dignity of an assumed order in things. Let me read you one poem by Anthony Hecht that illustrates this. It is titled, "'It Out-Herods Herod. Pray You Avoid It.'"—a quotation from an Elizabethan play.

> Tonight my children hunch
> Toward their Western, and are glad
> As, with a Sunday punch,
> The Good casts out the Bad.
>
> And in their fairy tales
> The warty giant and witch
> Get sealed in doorless jails
> And the match-girl strikes it rich.

I've made myself a drink.
The giant and witch are set
To bust out of the clink
When my children have gone to bed.

All frequencies are loud
With signals of despair;
In flash and morse they crowd
The rondure of the air.

Their very fund of strength,
Satan, bestrides the globe;
He stalks its breadth and length
And finds out even Job.

Yet by quite other laws
My children make their case;
Half God, half Santa Claus,
But with my voice and face,

A hero comes to save
The poorman, beggarman, thief,
And make the world behave
And put an end to grief.

And that their sleep be sound
I say this childermas
Who could not, at one time,
Have saved them from the gas.

Here is a poem of almost total cynicism and despair, yet Hecht finds it possible to seek for resolution in technical requirements alone, in that the poem by tradition must be rounded off. The prayer in the last stanza can only be construed as a premeditated token of helplessness. Yet all is well defined and orderly as a poem. The logic in life, death, and inhumanity relies upon the fulfillment of form. It is poetry, in a sense, that has run through its life already. It lacks confidence in any but the merest show of civilization, its outward form. It is the abandonment of self in confrontation with the giant odds, yet in its use of the traditional imposed form would demonstrate the continued steadfastness and viability of the past for the present. I can sympathize with this effort for what it is, an effort to make do. It is the marginal approach to life for many of us who lack anything else to rely on or with which to identify. Events are taken as they come in the helplessness to do anything about it. Hecht's poetry reflects this spirit, with a certain saving elegance. In their open, free forms, the vast majority of American poets take enormous risks with the psyche. Endless traps confront them, as Williams himself warned and as he experienced in his own continuous experimentation. The open form, the do-your-own-thing, he would often write, looks so simple and straightforward and so easily achieved through the mere abracadabra of words and sentences, arbitrarily, it would seem, out of one's hat. I shall take up this point again further on, in the conclusion to this talk. Before going on to other styles, however, I would like to note that Richard Wilbur, in the last poems of his I've read, appears as an exceptional instance of a traditional poet making the unusual effort to emerge in the direction of surrealism in free form.

At the extreme opposite pole of the Hecht poem is the single word poem of Aram Saroyan. This style originates in the dada movement of the post-World War I years, which, as with Williams, had the aim of overthrowing the fixed and regulated in the arts. In the case of dada, the aim was limited to presentations of the incongruous and the accidental, that which was incommunicable by the traditional rules of apprehension in a particular art. A Saroyan poem, for example, could be simply the word "IS" in the middle of a page. You might want to bring to it your past training and experience in poetry to assess the word as a poem, but Saroyan would reject and ridicule your presumption to judge his poem on the basis of your past training. It is *now* and it needs an entirely new approach. born of *now,* he would charge. You too are *now,* in all your confusions and urges and unformed ideas. You are IS. Williams would agree absolutely with this position, but would go on doing his own thing.

Between the extremes of dada and of formalism, and somehow absorbing the influences of both, is the poetry of Robert Creeley, one distinguished example. I would characterize his work as deeply *present* in tone. The language moves sparingly, almost discretely, as if the words were without connection each to each, filled with their own hesitance and tentativeness. This affecting poetry is a paradigm of the modern dilemma of our failure in relationships, and yet, as poetry, never lacks communication. especially in theme. At the conclusion of a particular poem, a kind of formality emerges, the inner personal dignity shaped by the movement and resolution of Creeley's thoughts. It's a poetry that has inspired a generation of younger poets to follow in its path.

A Reason

Each gesture
is a common one, a
black dog, crying, a
man, crying.

All alike, people
or things grow
fixed with what
happens to them.

I throw a stone.
It hits a wall,
it hits a dog,
it hits a child—

my sentimental
names for years
and years ago, from
something I've not become.

If I look
in the mirror,
the wall, I
see myself.

If I try
to do better
and better, I
do the same thing.

Let me hit you.
Will it hurt.
Your face is hurt
all the same.

To the left of Creeley, stylistically, is the poetry of
Robert Bly. Here is work charged with huge awakening
dreams, archetypal in character. It was meant that way.
Like Creeley's work, it too looks for hidden or miss-
ing links to one's identity, but in the applied Jungian
mode of the collective unconscious. Here is one recent
example.

Two Together

You open your mouth, I put my tongue in,
And this universe-thing begins!
Our tongues together are two seagulls whirling
        high above the Great Lakes,
Two jellyfish floating under a Norwegian moon!

Suddenly we are with the fallen leaves
        blowing along the soaked roads,
My hand closes so firmly around you
And I feel the sea rising and falling
        as I go ashore—

We are whirling together
     head down through oceans of space,
We are two turtles with wings,
We roll like tumbleweeds through the mother-air
     hurrying through the universe.

It's as mysterious after being read as before. It is wild and exciting, and yet its robust images and sounds are an assurance to us and to the poet of their beauty and goodness. Notice that the images are markedly discrete, one from the other, the connections left for the reader to make through overtones that arise in reading one image after the other. The principle is the same as that used by Creeley, and by Saroyan *in extremis,* but as language far exceeds anything that Creeley or Saroyan would attempt—or for that matter, even Williams, who advocated a primitive return. Bly's work has attracted an increasingly large following among new and more established poets in search of a way out—for example—of the negative humanism of Anthony Hecht's poetry.

We come next to the pattern poetry of Richard Kostelanetz, one of the more attractive poets in this style. It is related to the one word poem of Aram Saroyan, but Kostelanetz seeks to enhance and enlarge upon the word by shaping it on paper according to its actual significa-tion. For example, the word DISINTEGRATION is shown in successive stages of disintegration on the page. In effect, it nullifies the point of Saroyan's method and is actually a restatement of a style of writing as ancient as the earliest extant writing discovered. In practice, though, it derives from the Chinese ideogram introduced into American poetry by Ezra Pound. The Kostelanetz poem is also intimately connected with the very popular trend called concrete poetry. Kostelanetz would rather not call his work concrete, but it does have affinities, at least in principle. For example, in the word concrete itself, each letter could be shown on the page carved out of a huge block of masonry.

I'd like now to describe several styles that have grown principally out of their relationship to the conversational and to discourse. In a highly specialized sense, they are influenced by Williams's style, but Whitman is at the root of these developments—for Williams also. I refer first to the witty anecdotal poetry of Paul Blackburn. This hardly expresses the range of information, scholarly and experiential, that goes into these graceful lines. Blackburn is one of the leading authorities on Provençal poetry and thinking, but his own poetry is filled with daily intimate concerns, and their flavor of adventure and delight. Next in the poetry deriving from the art of the conversational is the para-ritual writing of Armand Schwerner. In his poems, the use of the conversational on all levels, fine, coarse, and explosive, is a deliberate effort to evoke an image of primitive man, man exposed to all the hazards of nature and to his own mystery. It is man conceived of in the beginning of his awareness, and his language projects just those primal confusions, awes, terrors, wonders, joys, and dawning insights, though not the physical deprivations and degradations to which he was then subject. This poetry probably is the farthest extension yet of Williams's dictum of the primitive, as it is basically oral poetry, but it has its sophistications and an ironical sense to it also. Schwerner's chief work, titled *The Tablets,* is among other things a parody, if not an absolute burlesque, of scholarly, intellectual presumptiveness. An authority in anthropological research serves as the butt. Schwerner is ridiculing the sort of detachment from reality, the so-called objectivity in academic communities, against which Williams fought so vigorously during his lifetime. This, though, is only one phase of *The Tablets,* and a means to a much more embracing, earthy celebration of life, at times wildly funny, more often embarrassing to our own hypocritical conditions.

We come next to the nonsequential Gertrude-Stein-like poetry of John Ashbery and Jerome Rothenberg, in which the phrases and sentences in common use among us are literally torn apart and placed in arbitrary relationships to one another, without regard to the intent of their original use. Now neither of these poets has any direct, perceptible relationship to the work or ideas of Williams or Whitman, and their poetry would seem to be the very opposite. Williams, in calling for a return to the primitive and unknowable in his poems, maintained the clarity of his surfaces. For Rothenberg and Ashbery, this clarity is the obstacle to their purposes. For example, the following passages from a sequence called "Sightings" by Jerome Rothenberg. A dot separates each sentence, and each sentence is on a line by itself, with the object of creating a silent pause between each. I will read the whole of "Sightings I."

He hides his heart.
.
A precious arrangement of glass and flowers.
.
They have made a covenant between them, the
circumstance of being tried.
.
Who will signal you?
.
It doesn't open to their touch though some
wait where it rests.
.
Try sleep.
.
The emblem perhaps of a herd of elephants—as signal
for a change of weather.
.
Animal.
.
A pigeon dreaming of red flowers.

In this sequence, Rothenberg would induce us to see new possibilities in ordinary sentences through an arrangement among them never before contemplated, with the purpose of lifting the ordinary and expected to a hitherto unexplored dimension of experience. It returns to the nonrational in us and rejects the cause and effect portrayal of reality to which we have been conditioned. Rothenberg's poems would replace this reality with an existence to him infinitely more complex and true than has been projected in the linear logic of our sciences and philosophies. Ultimately, the world of the subjective, the dark, the unformed and unpredictable to which he is urging us, is what he would name as the one certifiable reality in us all.

Among others writing from this perspective is David Antin. His wry manipulations expose the absurdity of relying on language itself for our grasp of reality. Jackson MacLow can be placed in relationship to Antin for his use of random techniques. This method employs words arbitrarily through chance selections from—for example—a dictionary opened with the eyes closed. In a poem published by MacLow in issue number 4-5 of the magazine *Some/Thing,* he has assembled a whole series of words, including nouns, adjectives, verbs, and participials, each through an intricate reasoning process derived from a musical score by Beethoven, *Bagatelle in B Minor, Op. 126.* Among those words and participials are "plate," "yearning," "generally," "generals," "felt," "platter." The poem is divided into seventy-two sections to correspond to the seventy-two measures in the Presto section of *Bagatelle.*

1. The plate?
A plate.

2. The plate ("a" plate?)
   generally
   felt like a "plate": generally?
   Generally.

3. Forty plates yearning,
   in general, for generals,
   yearning for forty
   generals, plateless generals,
   or ones who plateless felt.

4. If plateless, the generals felt
   (& generally,
   they felt, those generals, "plateless")
   was the generals' yearning
   felt?

This is not altogether a spoof of language and meaning. In fact, very wittily, the play on these random words has produced a comment on a particular point of view, and it may be concluded from the above that words can be made to say whatever you wish them to say, which falls in line with Antin's inferences, but the accidental and the incongruous of the dada movement are the keystones to this method. The results, though, are very different from the original plan. MacLow is saying something with which we can communicate instantly through our training and experience in past literatures. The difference from the past traditions is that MacLow is allowing himself full freedom of his mind to go where it will, in full confidence of the final results. The unconscious comes into play here equally with the unconscious of Robert Bly or Armand Schwerner, but of the order of MacLow's temperament and momentary disposition. The poem is actually metaphysical in tone and intent. I know I am raising questions in your minds by making such a flat statement about a revered intellectual tradition in connection with MacLow's ostensible confusion. I shall take up these questions along with others as the conclusion to my talk. I do want to go on to several more kinds of poetry circulating widely in this country, and having reputation outside the country too. Before going on, though, I want to comment briefly on the poetry of John Ashbery, who shares in the principles of Rothenberg, Antin, and MacLow, but enters a darkening area of experience, truly impenetrable and frightening in its most concentrated form. Here is a short poem in illustration.

Last Month

No changes of support—only
Patches of gray, here where sunlight fell.
The house seems heavier
Now that they have gone away.
In fact it emptied in record time.
When the flat table used to result
A match recedes, slowly, into the night.
The academy of the future is
Opening its doors and willing
The fruitless sunlight streams into domes,
The chairs piled high with books and papers.

The sedate one is this month's skittish one
Confirming the property that,
A timeless value, has changed hands.
And you could have a new automobile
Ping pong set and garage, but the thief
Stole everything like a miracle.
In his book there was a picture of treason only
And in the garden, cries and colors.

Note that the linear thinking here, beyond the first few sentences, suddenly and inexplicably veers off to give one a disoriented sense. It's as if one had been deliberately led down a path to enter a sudden maze, from which one is never to extricate oneself. The tone of self-assurance with which the poem proceeds in its baffling text becomes ominous for our own state of mind. Ashbery has a significant following among poets of a surrealist disposition in their own work.

A rather charming kind of poetry being "made" today, partaking of dada principles and the Williams free form, is that of the "found" poem. Here the poet takes a word, a sentence, a whole paragraph from magazines, books, newspapers, and advertising matter, without discernible relationship among them, and puts them together on a single page according to his or her insight into them as a group. Altogether, they say something different to us from their original purpose in print. It is a poet discovering possibilities for the sake of possibility. In other words, he is exercising his poetic talent for metaphor, relating the unrelated in unexpected, illuminating ways.

I am going to conclude this part of my talk by limiting myself to a group of the more notable styles that have caught on in this country and can be found in many anthologies and magazines. I am referring to a group of poets directly affected by Williams's own style. Its effect upon the poet is marked, though each poet's voice is distinctly his or her own. In this regard, Denise Levertov's work holds a central position. Confronting observed phenomena, she penetrates to their spiritual significance for her, much in accordance with Williams's own practice. Charles Reznikoff's objective presentations are straightforward comments upon themselves through subtle arrangements of their details. There is the intellectual dance among the parts by Louis Zukofsky, especially in his chief later work *A*, that is still in progress. There is George Oppen's definitive power and Harvey Shapiro's depths of somberness and elegiac control; the nature poetry of Gary Snyder, the jazz prosody of Ted Joans, the black folk idiom of Lucille Clifton, the city ironies of David Henderson, the jeremiads of LeRoi Jones, the exuberant metaphors of Simon Perchik. The poetry of Allen Ginsberg, Robert Lowell, Galway Kinnell, Louis Simpson, John Berryman, and W. S. Merwin, to name a few of the more prominent, has been described and discussed knowingly and at length elsewhere by others—some of these poets also owing a debt to Williams, others hardly so. But everyone in this vast, ever proliferating diversification serves to emphasize over and over the deeply subjective phenomenon among us called poetry, and all of it, by tacit understanding among the poets themselves, accepted as poetry.

How could this be, we ask, with each poet so much himself, uniquely different in makeup and point of view from the others? I am talking about the open, free form and the dada influence in their infinite variety. For the reader alone it could be a baffling experience, leading him to contrary and conflicting opinions about poems vastly different from each other. Obviously, this tacit understanding among the poets is in rejection of any objective criterion for poetry. But do we actually have an objective criterion? This is the question I have raised in my discussion of the numerous styles developed by poets with roots in the dada and free form movements.

There is no objective criterion for the judgment of poetry. An Anthony Hecht might insist on a technical basis for his own grounds, but as we have seen, these grounds have been rejected by American poets as a whole, among whom we can count national prize winners, university professors, and poets with international reputation. There is no objective criterion as such for the judgment of the truly contemporary poem, certainly not in the traditional sense that a poem must adhere to a set of rules before it can be judged for the proficiency of its conduct. How then can we examine the work being done in the name of poetry? How can we praise that which is done? Are we in a dilemma? What criterion are we using in praising the poets today and encouraging them in their efforts? For me, the question simply returns to the first underlying principle in modern poetry since before T. S. Eliot, and in agreement with him—precisely the principle which puts Eliot and Williams in secret affinity with each other. This is the principle stated by Williams in his 1936 article, from which I have already quoted, "How to Write," and which, unquestionably, was not an original discovery with him either, given the intellectual climate of the 1920s in which he matured.

The subjective is all that is real for the person, meaning each and every one of us. In the poem, it is the expression of one's reality, something we must respect at once. There is no contravening another person's sense of himself and his world. We must accept it on his terms, though we need not accept it for ourselves. But this is not an impasse in the art of poetry. It is actually a fantastic discovery of unlimited possibilities. Men and women have discovered themselves as individuals, and that this sense of individuality is something shared among them as a way of life. Paradoxically, it is a way of life that leads to community. In affirming themselves, they affirm all the others. It is the discovery of free relationships within community. But how do we derive poetry from this discovery? Poetry, as I see it, is formed by the terms with which the person sees himself. These are terms embodied in his poems. They are the terms by which he lives and by which his poems must gain their authenticity, first of all. They are terms as they originate in and flow from insights into his life; and this is no different from what Wallace Stevens, a contemporary of Williams and a friend, has said in his book, *Ideas of Order*—to paraphrase, What the imagination does with the reality we are is the reality we live by. Let me quote the last six lines of a poem, "The Truth," by Pablo Neruda, the greatest of the South American poets, and counted among the greatest in the world.

> speak your secret in secret;
> and to truth: never withhold what you know
> lest you harden the truth in a lie.
>
> I am no one's establishment. I administer
> nothing: it suffices to cherish
> the equivocal cut of my song.

Doesn't this remind you of Whitman? Well, Neruda has named Whitman as the father of his inspiration from the very start. No doubt, the point I have raised as to the authenticity and wholeness of modern poetry is complicated, but its principles are clear: they are rooted in being. As individuals, we live unto ourselves. This has been forced on us by our divided and conflicting culture. As poets, then, we first affirm ourselves as persons. As with everyone else, it is vitally important that we know who we are and where we are in a society that is in constant motion and counter motion. To be caught up in this conflict without a firm grasp of oneself is to invite destruction, indiscriminate and impersonal. This is what each of us refuses to let happen, and so the poet, reacting in like manner, makes that effort to be identified with himself and others. He does it with the poem. He sets himself apart from his society and its maelstrom in the poem. He distinguishes himself from the threatening chaos with the poem that says who he is, what he is thinking. The reader finds a distinct life style in the work, a sense of self separate from and in relation to the environment. The poet cannot be confused with anyone else. He has absorbed his time and place, and yet retains his own identity. It is the affirmation of being. It is the principle of free form.

This is the mind of the serious poet, and it separates him decisively from all previous traditions in the history of his art. It has links with the dada movement but goes beyond it in affirming once more an order to things—but in one's own being. It affirms the power and uniqueness of the person. It emphasizes the individual as judge of his own acts, including his art. It forces others to look upon his acts and his art in terms of his own making. At the same time, it makes the poet responsible for the integrity of his poems in terms of his being. This is the principle by which the contemporary poem may be judged for its value as a poem, in my view. It is consistent with the autonomy of the person as poet and makes both reader and writer search out, each for himself, that inner coherence which is the mark of the free form.

As a principle, it is not easy to live up to steadily for the poet, nor is it any easier for the reader to apply, for all his patience and empathy with the poet and his poems. A tragic example of such a relationship was the one between Ralph Waldo Emerson and Walt Whitman. It is to Whitman that we owe this principle of the autonomy of the poet, but Emerson in his later years found it impossible to accept, after having hailed Whitman in the early years as the genius he was looking for in American letters. Whitman in his later poems had become even more explicitly himself, to Emerson's horror. In 1876, compiling a comprehensive anthology of American poets then writing, Emerson deliberately left out Whitman. Through all of Emerson's complaints about him ran the recurrent one about Whitman's supposedly obscene self-exposure in the later poems, against all canons of society. Whitman refused to accommodate himself to those canons by cutting or omitting the offensive poems, and Emerson disowned him. Today there is even less room than before for accommodation. First of all, we have discovered that we ourselves are this society and, as such, we cannot compromise without bringing disaster upon ourselves and the country which is ours. We must persevere and maintain ourselves on this high level of commitment. We no longer have a choice. As poets, we are making our own destiny. It no longer can be imposed on us from outside, as in the past. Influences there will always be, but to be used at our discretion. There once was a call among American critics for that epic poet who would tell the story of this country straight and whole. That story is being told now, poet by poet, a clear, loud, and very powerful truth.

1971

L. C. Woodman

A Personal Memory

I think of Lawrence as dead, surrounded by his manu-
scripts, books, newspaper clippings, correspondence, and
phonograph records, all heaped in piles like rubbish on
the floor of his apartment. He is found lying in the over-
sized, crumpled suit that he had bought at a Salvation
Army Depot for pennies spared from his old-age pension.
In this cold-water flat off the Bowery there is no furni-
ture, a mattress on the floor serves as a bed, and Lawrence
is found alone, for no one had been able to get behind
his jovial eccentricity to help him.

Born into a New Hampshire farming family, Lawrence
Chauncey Woodman was raised first by his father and
then by relatives on his mother's side. His mother died
three weeks after his birth. Years later he was to write
over a thousand poems to her memory, blaming himself
for her death. His father, hard-pressed on the farm with-
out her, could not stop reminding Lawrence of her
death. Then, when Lawrence was just over four years
old, his father boarded him out with his mother's sister
on whose husband's farm the boy was put to work in
fields and barns from sunrise to sunset.

When he was six he was sent to school, a welcome es-
cape. There he made the most of his leisure in dreaming
about his mother and the life they might have had to-

gether. His thoughts were not on his lessons, and almost everything he learned he soon forgot—except how to read and write. Of all his studies he took only words seriously; they clothed his deepening thoughts about his mother, that one obsessive theme with which almost everything he wrote from then on had to do. About his father he wrote bitterly in his school compositions, accusing him of kicking and cursing him. He soon began to make these feelings known to his father too. On his father's rare visits, Lawrence would come out of his room reluctantly, and he would be adamant in his refusal to go home with his father during holidays. Between the two a hostile silence grew during the years.

Lawrence continued to live with his aunt and uncle on their farm, earning his keep by working after school until he was old enough to leave for Bates College. There he worked his way, too, waiting on tables and doing janitorial work. Lawrence was short and thin and it was very difficult for him to keep up with his studies, haul ash barrels from the cellar, scrub floors—but out of something like despair in the little time he had for leisure he managed to distinguish himself on the school baseball team. His writing, meanwhile, was marked more and more by violent rebellion alternating with extravagant dreams of loving and being loved. Shelley and Keats were his two idols. At graduation Lawrence was recognized as an emotional and perhaps unstable but brilliant writer who was headed for great fame.

His instability was to have disastrous consequences in his subsequent career. Jobs on national weekly magazines would explode under the stress of his unregulated, uncontrolled conduct. An assigned subject in which he found it difficult to maintain interest he would shape to his own personal use, interpolating private asides of no meaning to the reader, or suddenly beginning to play at verbal pyrotechnics describing his loneliness. Often, ignoring the assignment entirely, he would go directly into his own immediate private problems. His writing would be filled with the pathos of a man still seeking relief from the griefs of his childhood, but the language would be high-pitched and hysterical, bordering on the irrational. In his excitement he would forget about deadlines. Admonished, warned and blue-penciled time and again, eventually he would be dropped from the staff, to the deep puzzlement and repugnance of his superiors.

For Lawrence, each failure reinforced his belief that he was cut out not to be a professional man of letters but to be a poet, one who must express his innermost feelings at any cost. Because he saw every occasion for writing as an opportunity to tell his own story, it was not long before he had exhausted the list of local professional literary magazines to which he could apply for jobs. His search took him across country, and with him went the wife of a farmer. Besides leaving her husband, she was also separating from another man—a tall, dark-haired husky truck driver who was married and reluctant to leave with her. Lawrence managed to overcome her own reluctance to part from the trucker and from her husband by his passionate conviction that together he and she could find compensation for their mutual griefs against all stiff-necked, arrogant farmers. It was apparent to her, and to Lawrence too for that matter, that they were going almost as mother and child. The poems he had been writing her were worshipful as of some unattainable ideal. Charmed and perhaps touched by such adoration, she took Lawrence to her with a maternal love, leaving behind three children of her own.

At the other end of the country, the distance they had put between them and her husband served also to loosen their common bond. On the farm as a hard-worked wife up at dawn to be burdened by children and chores until sundown, she had felt justified in wanting to run away, but now the thousands of miles dividing her from husband and children gave her guilt feelings. Lawrence spent his days away from her working in the basement of a department store as stock clerk, barely supporting them both, while at night he shut himself in his room to write her worshipful poems. Things were no better for her here than at home. She left him.

Lawrence sorrowfully went about seeking to rebuild his career without her. This time he decided on teaching and returned to Columbia to work for his master's degree. Dishwashing for a living during the day, he did eventually succeed in winning his degree but not without the pity and help of his professor. In Lawrence the professor saw an extraordinary personality capable of fantastic flights of the imagination. Lawrence employed his thesis subject, the poetry of Robert Frost, as a platform from which to launch a violent attack on Puritanism, against which he set his own vision of life, of unlimited possibilities for love and happiness between men and women and between men without shame, guilt, or reservation, a vision that could be realized almost at once if men would only turn from preconceived, narrow, stultified ideas and let life come into them through their uninhibited senses.

In Lawrence, the professor recognized a true romantic who needed only to forge a certain clarity and direction with which to convince others. Over and over he had Lawrence revise his writing for coherence and relevance toward Frost's poems, only to realize finally that this was a goal Lawrence would never achieve. Out of pity, concerned with him as a person whom he found far too excitable for his own good, he certified Lawrence for his degree, but with strong private forebodings about his future teaching career.

It was not long after that the pattern established in Lawrence's literary career began to assert itself in his teaching jobs. Always the start would be brilliant, only to explode in disorder and emotional fireworks, charges and countercharges between him and his superiors. The first week of regular teaching according to curriculum would be carried off with clarity and force. By the middle of the second week clarity would vanish in the excitement of dreams and rebellion. Girl students would begin to hear themselves addressed in class with a kind of idealistic passion. After class, alone with a girl student, who would stay behind for additional instructions or out of curiosity or titillation, Lawrence would dare to make love to her with hands and voice. During later classes, he would boldly request her to stay again, to the knowing titters of the rest. He would harangue male students against their elders, against the rigid discipline and conventions forced on them through parental and incidentally academic authority, all of which to Lawrence was the result of a callous disregard of the true spirit of creativity that should be in learning. Lawrence preached that in the hidebound atmosphere at home and at school one had to rebel simply to be oneself, and he would set the example by throwing aside the required course of studies for the class and preach the virtues of friendship, love, and shared sorrows. In class, Lawrence and the girl student to whom he would be attached at the time would exchange knowing looks.

The influence of his ideas would spread like a tidal wave through the English department; method would drown in excited discourse among students on the need to practice that rapport among themselves that was to be derived from a true interpretation of the books. Out of gratitude to Lawrence for awakening them to a new and fresh view of life, students would form intense attachments to him. He would be overjoyed—but he would be losing his job. On one memorable occasion, to his thrilled astonishment, the students of Washington College (Maryland) drew up a petition to protest his being fired. The protest received national attention and Lawrence received an offer of an editorial job on the Baltimore *Sun,* one newspaper that had strongly supported the petition. In those days, it was a sensation for students to abandon discipline and decorum over issues raised by a teacher's being dismissed on charges of inefficiency and immoral teaching.

Lawrence applied for the editorial job, but that too vanished because of his insistence on writing in his per-fervid style only of what excited him. Through every-thing, Lawrence continued to write his poems at top speed. He also had begun to write short stories and plays on the obsessive theme of his parents. His father repre-sented all that was evil and hypocritical in New England life. His mother, who Lawrence now saw as having died of callous neglect on his father's part, he portrayed as a gentle victim like himself. His prose style by now had changed significantly. He no longer made an effort to communicate directly with his reader. He now believed it necessary for him to follow every intricacy of his thought in order to get at the complete picture. Henceforth, where necessary, he would abandon logical and gram-matical correctness to get at the full development of his theme. He would try to reproduce the true state of his mind, to create an image of absolute authenticity, to bring life at its fullest to the reader. Years later, he would claim to have anticipated James Joyce's use of the stream of consciousness.

While teaching, Lawrence managed to get himself married to a widow with one child. He had been intro-duced to her in New York during his summer vacation, by his friend and cousin Joe Gould. Almost at once, he conceived a passion for her. Her foreign accent and her past tragic experiences as a Russian emigré struck a responsive chord in him who too felt an outcast in his own country. Their marriage was the start of the most harrowing ten years of their lives.

As if to voice his defiance anew, now that he was married and a responsible man, Lawrence made more and louder declarations against the narrow and rigid academic curriculum and against conventions in general. He enthusiastically collected stories, poems, and essays by students writing under his influence (now at Coe College in Iowa) and published them in book form at his own expense. The anthology was named *Contemporaries,* it made a favorable impression on reviewers, and it was full of pieces on love, life, and literature, all written in accordance with Lawrence's exhortations that the student writers be uninhibited. As a result of this perhaps, and as a result of Lawrence's ever more violent and demonstrative behavior in class and among the faculty, Lawrence was discharged in the middle of term without terminal pay after a red-faced quarrel with his department chairman who had criticized him for rejecting the class course of study in favor of his own brand of teaching.

Fired, with no immediate prospects of a job ahead, he took his wife and stepdaughter into the country to set up housekeeping in an abandoned farmhouse, and for almost two years lived on money borrowed from her artist brother and on food begged and cajoled from neighboring farmers. Back in New Hampshire, his own two older brothers completely ignored all appeals from him for aid. Through the estate lawyer Lawrence heard of his father's death. A small but solid inheritance of two farms had been left to his brothers but no provision nor even mention had been made of Lawrence in the will.

By now Lawrence was forty years old and in deep

distress. He had failed as a teacher. He had almost no reputation as a writer. He had ruined his career as journalist and he could not again try to work for the literary magazines. All that remained was book reviewing or reading for publishers, neither of which paid well nor could add to his prestige. It was not until two bitter winters had gone past in that half-torn-down farmhouse that Lawrence got promise of a steady job as a publisher's reader and of being given books for review in New York newspapers. This job came through the good offices of Lawrence's professor mentor back in New York, and on the strength of it, with money advanced by his wife's brother, Lawrence brought his family to an attic apartment in Brooklyn. It was the beginning of a daily round of hack work. Through his position as book reader with one publisher, he obtained extra work from other houses. In the New York *Sun* he reviewed, anonymously, *A Portrait of the Artist as a Young Man* and *Dubliners,* both of which he virtually hailed as masterpieces. He had been excited to find similarities with his own even more radical style, on which he looked with pardonable pride as even in advance of Joyce. But it was all soon to be submerged in the steady grind to make a passable living for his family and self. No one single job was sufficient to cover his expenses and it was not long before he began to tire and grow irritable and excited about his hardships. Much as he feared the return of those bleak, desperate days on the abandoned farm, he was unable to control his mounting sense of injustice. Once more his work began to show signs of waywardness, interpolations of sharp criticisms in the midst of straight puffs for commercial best sellers. This would regularly have to be cut out by the editorial desk and the review fitted together as coherently as possible. Again he would commit the cardinal sin of bringing in copy three or four days late, and he was released from newspaper reviewing gently after several months, with promises of books more suited to his "sophisticated" tastes if and when these books arrived.

Lawrence did not take this without strong, excited protest. It marked the absolute end of his career as a book reviewer. At the same time, his various reading jobs for publishers began significantly to dwindle. He had been filling his evaluations with quotations from the writings of other authors on the same subject, in disparagement of the manuscript under consideration. Also he had begun to make his reading an opportunity to sound off on his own aesthetic beliefs as opposed to the work in hand, in hopes it would encourage the publisher to go out and look for such work, perhaps that of Lawrence. Soon his reading jobs dwindle to one or two a month, hardly enough to pay the food bill. By now Lawrence was thought of by editors as somewhat off balance and of little use to them in their work. Finally, the one or two books a month sank to none.

It was also the time of the Great Depression, which lent a semblance of truth to the plea of the need for economy on the part of the publishers who had dropped Lawrence from their payrolls. Lawrence, however, was not so insulated as not to realize that he had contributed to his own downfall through professionally inadmissable acts, and he began to look upon himself as a failure. All that was left for him now was Home Relief. By this time, his wife too had surmised the kind of man she had married and had returned to the seamstress work with which she had been supporting herself before marriage. Relations between them as man and wife had been nonexistent since their stay at the abandoned farm. Lawrence cooked for himself his own purchases of food, while she cooked for her daughter and herself. His ways had become repugnant to her. He would buy dangerously rusty and crushed cans of food for pennies from some push-cart peddler, dump the contents of several cans into a pot, whether they were sardines, meat, vegetable, or pudding, and boil the mess for several hours and then store it on a shelf of the icebox for several weeks, making a meal of it from time to time, as the fancy took him. He would repeat this operation two or three times a month, adding more pots to the shelf and crowding out the sensible things his wife would buy from day to day, fresh and normally priced. The icebox leaked and was never cold enough and the contents of the pots would begin to rot and stink. He would simply cut away those rotting parts and make a meal for himself of the remainder. During one climactic argument with his wife, she settled any illusion he might have had about her love and approbation by letting him know that she bitterly regretted the marriage which in any case she had gone through merely for the sake of the child who needed a father and a home, but since he was a fool and not even a good writer she was through with him. In spluttering anguish, as she completed listing her contempt for him, he challenged her judgment of him and shouted his defiance of her and his belief in himself as a great writer, but in the silence of her disdain his shouting died down into a cold exchange between them on the need to continue to live together to facilitate their application for relief.

After less than five years of marriage she had grown completely grey. The large blue eyes that Lawrence had admired when they were first married were now wrinkled and squinting behind thick-lensed glasses with which she sewed for strangers under the night lamp after a day's house work. For Lawrence, the situation in which he found himself now had become unbearable too. Surrounded by the hostility of his wife and stepdaughter, he felt himself sinking into a deathlike oblivion. The little girl whom he had adopted with such compassion and pride also acted with contempt toward him, influenced by her mother. She would run away from him to hide in her room when he approached with a gift or an offer to read to her from the children's classics.

Out of desperation, disguising his name from Home Relief officials who might be looking for just such a move as he now conceived, Lawrence contrived to hire a hotel room for an evening each week and to advertise it as the meeting place for a new "Independent Writers" group, dedicated to free, creative work. The idea came to him in a return to the memory of his past difficult glory as a college teacher. The money to advertise he filched from the family bimonthly relief check. Every second week he would run downstairs ahead of his wife to the mailbox to remove the Welfare Department money voucher addressed to him as head of the family. He would run with it to the nearest bank, cash it, and take for his share a few more pennies than he was entitled to. With a rare small check that he got for manuscript reading from time to time, after hard begging, he would then have provided himself with the hotel room rent and the cost of the ad. At the start, enough curiosity seekers and earnest students of writing would turn up to pay back his expenses and sometimes he would be left with a few extra dollars for the next meeting. He would be a proud, excited man.

His contacts among the bohemian writers in the Village supplied the necessary flavor to his meetings. Each week he trotted out a different celebrity who would perform in his or her characteristic manner. Among them were Joe Gould, Maxwell Bodenheim, and John Rose Gildea. Lawrence had gotten to know them all from sitting around with them in their cafés. He got along well with them. As a former college teacher who had been exiled, so to speak, for his intransigence, they looked on him with favor, though with condescension, for they had declared themselves rebels long before his disillusion with the moral and spiritual tone of society. Lawrence respected them for having been even more prescient than he in their approach to the world. But these friends had to be paid for appearing at his meetings. That left him less money than he had hoped for, but his pleasure and pride in having organized a literary group along lines of his own thinking compensated for the financial lack. At these hotel meetings, he felt free to expound at length on his theories of writing. He believed vehemently in a realism that left nothing unsaid or undone. He rejected all squeamishness. In balance, he believed too in the fantasy and poetry that could spring from these very facts, and to cite examples of what he meant he would recite passages from the English romanticists, mixing in passages from his own poems. He would stop to ask what they thought of that particular stanza and invariably he would get approving nods or words of praise, in the belief by the audience that he was reciting unfamiliar passages from the accepted classics. Lawrence would shy away from telling outright it was his writing but keep a sly knowing smile on his round, florid face as he read. Also he would read from Hemingway or Joyce or Stein to give his audience a taste of realism, and here too he would mix in paragraphs from his own writings, but proudly identify them as his own.

The fact that he held in him two mutually exclusive theories of writing, that of fantasy and that of realism was to be understood in the master theory that they were interchangeable through the very nature of life itself in all its unpredictable variety. Further, by this very adaptableness, they could make a story or poem or play authentic and perhaps great with the proper use of each or both elements, depending upon the author's mind. He would cite Joyce for examples of successful use of both methods in one work and then would go on to read his own writings to show a further and even more radical and successful extension of his theory. In astonishment, his listeners would be half persuaded by the audacity of his claim, especially since almost nothing of what he read of his own work could be understood, at least on first hearing. As to be expected, words, syntax, ideas, and narrative sequences would be at odds with one another in the text, but he would slur his delivery in the paroxysms of rage or ecstasy that would grip him in those passages he considered appropriate to the mood. These readings and lectures would form the introduction to the evening and the rest of the night would be spent listening to the recital of poems or prose by one of Lawrence's Village guests. Perhaps later in the evening, if there were time, he would solicit manuscripts from the audience to be read aloud by the writer then and there. He would then publicly encourage manuscripts written from his point of view. He could even tolerate other work in order to encourage writers he thought had something that lent itself to his view. At other times, when the going was heavy and slow, the writing lacking in spirit and insight, he would place the palm of his hand to his mouth from time to time to stifle a yawn.

At each of these meetings, Lawrence acted as the ex-college professor whose integrity and talent had led to his downfall and exile from academia. He had begun to collect and preserve his newspaper and periodical reviews for which formerly he had so little respect. In each he could see the germ of his emerging thought, although muted and garbled by the editorial hand. He also had as concrete evidence the letter from the newspaper publisher at the time the students had drawn up their petition for him. He exhibited the letter as vindication of his struggle against the reactionary academic world and he used it regularly to establish his respectability with each new audience. For those who had begun to attend regularly, this was thought of as an obligation on his part to explain and identify himself before a hostile world. These few "regulars" had much in common with the students who had used to attach themselves to Lawrence. Among them were several commercial writers who had begun to skid because of drink and were writing with marked eccentricity as compared with their former straight hack prose. Lawrence counted on this nucleus for the expense of the hotel room and the ad.

All the while, the Welfare Department was to have no way of uncovering this club. Lawrence did not use his name in advertisements of the meetings. Besides, his past record of employment did not lead them to think that he was capable of organizing and sustaining such a large group. In their reports, he was listed as psychologically unemployable. On the other hand, he had acquired a kind of preeminence in the Village itself. Attendance at his meetings had grown to an average of thirty-five, and each meeting now was regularly marked by a flare-up of temperament among members whose manuscripts were being criticized by others. Over it all, Lawrence presided with high good humor, out of pride at being the originator of the club itself and incidentally on the way to making some money.

When the Welfare Department did catch up with him, it was in a most surprising way. Those were the days of the start of the WPA projects in all fields, including education and the arts. Lawrence on the basis of his record was assigned to a teaching project in creative writing, with a definite place, schedule, and curriculum of study. No one could have been more delighted and frightened than Lawrence. He could recall his past disastrous experiences with fixed courses of study. He was more than afraid that these experiences would repeat themselves. In fact, the classes being organized were modeled after the established courses given in colleges and based on Dean Howells and Thackeray, neither of whom Lawrence could tolerate. On the other hand, he felt vindicated by the recognition given him as a former college teacher.

His first act was to give up the "Independent Writers" group, after which events moved much as he had feared. He was required to take a refresher course in the techniques of teaching as offered by distinguished pedagogues from equally distinguished schools. Lawrence was apprehensive about this, but he feared even more being cut off from relief. His first teaching sessions at a neighborhood community center where the classes were taking place were complete flops. He did his best to follow the program laid out for him by the pedagogues, but the students began to stay away in droves. Lawrence taught in a toneless, sing-song delivery. Nothing of himself was involved. He spoke entirely from rote, delivering his speeches as he recalled their being spoken for him by the instructors, and he would give assignments to write coherent paragraphs at home to be brought to class for the examination of their syntax, subject matter, and development of idea. He was in despair. By the third week, the class was down to three students staring at him with blank looks. Sensing an almost certain loss of his job as a result, he threw aside all caution and began using his own brand of instruction. In any case, he was too distraught to do anything now but talk about himself. It was exactly how he had started out with the "Independent Writers." Gradually his class began to fill up again and once more a nucleus formed around him, strikingly identical with all the others before.

So long as he did not have to fear a visit by his supervisor, he exulted over his new success and visualized himself at the center of the literary world again. He felt confident and strong enough to continue with a program of magazine publishing he had started back in the "Independent Writers" group. Two magazines already had been published by him, with much of the material by his students and himself; the first issues of *Literary Arts* and *American Scene* had been well received. Now Lawrence resolved to put out the second issues of *Literary Arts* and *American Scene* and the first issues of two new magazines, *Idiom* and *Womenkind*. *Womenkind* would consist of work by women only, out of respect for their talents and in protest against the prejudice and exploitation they suffered at the hands of men. It was also intended to attract women readers and earn a good, steady profit. All the magazines, however, were part of his grand scheme to reeducate the American writer and American public in the arts of writing and reading and living.

In class, Lawrence boasted that he had become the most ambitious and inventive editor in the field, proving his theory that a man allowed full freedom of expression could contribute vitally to the liberty and equality of the people. However, he was cautious in warning his students not to expect immediate publication in his magazines. For the time being he had his eye on those writers whose work had caught his eye elsewhere and who already had reputations. He meant to gather under one banner the strongest possible influence upon American life and literature. This would also give him a chance to publish his own works in the context he thought suitable for them—with that of his peers.

Fired by this vision of becoming the spokesman of American literature, his first practical step was to purchase a secondhand mimeograph machine and install it in his apartment. Here was another venture that his wife looked on with cold disdain. She had no faith in his ability to achieve anything worthwhile and resented his spending money for the machine, and for paper, ink, and postage. It would all have to come out of his WPA salary, while she continued to sew for strangers to supplement his meager earnings. He set up the machine in his bedroom where each morning he cranked out the pages, after typing their stencils with one finger. Copies of mimeographed pages began to overflow into the living room and kitchen and this became another sore point between his wife and him. His resentment of her grew more pronounced with each new squabble over the "mess" and "dirt" he made with his machine. He would threaten to leave for good and she would coolly invite him to do so. By now, feverish with dreams of literary reknown as he worked day and night at this machine, he felt sustained in turning to the female side of his class for comfort and approbation. His attention was fixed upon a tall, sallow-faced, pockmarked woman who by her physical appearance, especially by the suggestion of red in her hair, reminded him of his earlier love, the farmer's wife. He had been told as a child that the color of his mother's hair had been red, like his own. Mrs. Cantwell, in her early thirties, was not unattractive as she entered the class at the beginning of a period. Slim but shapely, she would be dressed in a formfitting suit or dress and would carry herself with grave dignity to her chair at the study table. During class, she would listen solemnly attentive to Lawrence's lecturing on modern writing. He would read from his own unpublished works, partly to impress Mrs. Cantwell, but also to have them serve as models for his students to follow. These were the stories he intended to publish in his magazines.

He also kept his class informed of his daily progress

in getting material from known writers. His correspondence from all over the country had indeed suddenly grown large and he had more to do actually than he could handle, but he was delighted by it. He would enter class with packages of manuscripts and letters piled high in his arms. It was as impressive to his students as it was to Mrs. Cantwell. She was aiming to become a children's story writer and Lawrence's success as an editor could only mean a better opportunity for herself. He began to walk her home after class, and they would discuss many things, particularly his consuming interest in her. She was quite reserved about that. She was especially reserved about certain overtones in his stories treating of relations between men and women. From what she could gather through the dense, devious language, the hero (a hardly disguised Lawrence) was the sort of man who could not be tied down to one way of living. The stories were intended to put the hero's restless habits in an adventurous light, as if it were his god-given duty to create problems in place of silence and calm. To Mrs. Cantwell, this was no way for a married man to act and she was quite plain-spoken about it as they walked together. It was, she noted, the kind of behavior which had led her to divorce her husband, and now to find it in Lawrence also, who was much more gifted spiritually than her husband, was a deep disappointment indeed. Lawrence took all this as a challenge. At her apartment he would try to slide past her as she stood in the doorway, but her firm, dignified arm would restrain him, together with the shocked tones of her voice questioning his motives. She was a lady born and bred in the gentlemanly traditions of the Old South and expected men to live up to these traditions wherever they were. Lawrence would back away, grumbling but apologetic and would leave more determined than ever to break down her reserve. In class, his students were tolerant and even amused by his open attentions to her. It added vividness to his teaching. They felt they had so much more to learn from him than at first they had realized concerning the open and courageous posture toward life that he preached.

Nothing was to come of this romance. Mrs. Cantwell never once let him past into her apartment. Nor would she discuss love with him in their walks home together except in a most objective, didactic way. Several times, over his most fervent protestations, she had to tell him matter of factly that she did not love him in the least. As they walked, Lawrence's arms would be piled high with books, letters, bags of oranges, apples, and vegetables. He would dip into an open bag of cookies perched on top of the heap in his arms and bring one to his mouth to chew on excitedly. He was short and fat. He would have to trot to keep up with the tall, long-legged, somber Mrs. Cantwell. Over and over as he pressed himself upon her she would tell him gravely in measured tones that a man first had to prove himself to her before she could think of love. Her broken marriage had taught her that much about love.

All this Lawrence used as an excuse for finally leaving his wife and taking an apartment in Mrs. Cantwell's neighborhood. With him he took his truckload of books, newspaper clippings, manuscripts, phonograph records, bedding, clothes, and the few pieces of furniture he claimed as his own from the days before marriage—a single bed, a desk, a phonograph, a typewriter, the mimeograph machine, a leather chair, and a chest of drawers. These were to form the beginning of a new home, at least for himself, if not yet for Mrs. Cantwell. He meant to keep trying. He would have the apartment ready for her when at last her resistance was melted. He believed it still possible, if only because she could discuss the issue with him at all. In this resided his hope. In this lay his fate as a writer. During his affair with the farmer's wife, he had written poems and stories by the dozen. It was most urgent now that he get Mrs. Cantwell to live with him, to fall in love with him, if he was to write again as he had in that great outburst of former years.

Mrs. Cantwell was not moved. Several years went by. Lawrence made his monthly visit to his grey-haired and by now nearly blind wife, to leave with her her share of his WPA salary. She would hold out her hand in silence, indifferently. It confirmed as nothing else could his need for a love that could measure up to a man of his talent. By this time, three of his magazines had been published and distributed. *Idiom* had been postponed for lack of money and time. Comments mainly favorable were coming in from all over. Delighted with himself, he was convinced of his place in the literary scene. Already he could visualize the makeup of subsequent issues. Enough copy had come in, but he was pressed for money. Sales were few in those Depression years. Authors themselves were writing him asking for loans and extra free copies of the magazines. He was spending his surplus cash to keep up his apartment in Mrs. Cantwell's neighborhood. He still was persuaded of his chances. He could feel a strong pulse of attraction to him beneath her austere surface. It took the form of regular, grave criticisms of his dress, manners, and occasional off-color jokes. To Lawrence, her behavior toward him reminded him of nothing so much as of the farmer's wife, if only because she too used to constantly criticize him.

In the meanwhile, the class had grown noisy and disorderly. Exhilarated over the critical success of his magazines, he had been professing with even more passion than ever his own creed of instinctive emotional writing. Also, he kept his frustrating love affair out in the open in front of the class with repeated jokes and asides to Mrs. Cantwell. Students would enter drunk, rowdy, or argumentative. Beggars would wander in off the streets, somewhere, somehow having heard of a very liberal, warm-hearted teacher at the head of a convival group of drinkers and lovebirds. Lawrence would then have to spend most of the time pleading with these men to leave so as not to jeopardize his job. Unhappy, depressed women would wander in, fixed upon some hallucinatory grievance or vision. It would be even more difficult to get rid of them. They would enter and sit down silently and unobtrusively for a while and then later suddenly burst out with their obsessions. Lawrence, appalled, would try to hush them, but was too shocked and moved to act sternly. One such woman began to attach herself regularly to his class, and her arrival would be the signal for some of his more conventional students to get up and leave. At moments, real pandemonium would break out in class. Lawrence would be shouting at the top of his lungs trying to control the deranged woman while the students, gasping and frightened, would be scrambling out of the room and making a great racket with their chairs.

One day Lawrence did manage to get rid of the un-balanced woman by a strategem, sending her with his most kindly advice to a class in grammar by way of pre-paration for a talented career in writing. It was an irony that did not escape Lawrence, but he was desperate; in-cidents of this sort were happening much too regularly and he had begun to feel a distinct coolness toward him on the part of Mrs. Cantwell. She was beginning to stay away for several days at a time. Lawrence himself was beginning to realize that it was not much to his credit to be teaching an odd collection of drunks, beggars, and deranged women. This was not as he had visualized his class, free of conventional restraint but bent on a kind of freedom that released one to write and live with spirit and joy. Teaching here seemed to have reduced itself to being a watch warden of manners and language, if he were to stay on the government payroll. He might have brought order into his class, at the risk of losing virtually the entire attendance. He would have to refuse admission to men and women carrying bottles into class and to others who came simply to flirt, make dates, and talk among themselves and to others who sat sullen and silent through the entire period, but to have refused admission would in some undefined way have been a violation of his own most private instincts. He felt a deep identity with them all, and wished not to hurt or insult them, for fear it might somehow return to hurt him. In despair, he struggled with his problem each night, seeking order with appeals to caution and with occasional jokes to relieve the tension of men and women lifting bottles to their lips in class. He would throw harried glances at the door, in momentary expectation of the worst, his supervisor. In the meanwhile, he continued reading from submitted manuscripts in the midst of babble and laughter, with exhortations on the need for the personal touch in everything.

When Mrs. Cantwell did show up, Lawrence would act hurt and angry and would make a point of paying no attention to her but deliberately address himself to some other woman, joking and teasing with her. It was with the hope of making Mrs. Cantwell jealous so as to stir her to some positive gesture toward him, but after class she would make preparations to leave without him, gathering her belongings together without so much as a glance in his direction. In anguish, Lawrence would rush up to the door as she was about to close it behind her and ask if he could accompany her home. Gravely, she would refuse his company. He would try to make her promise to return the next night, and she would refuse. Lawrence grew irritable with himself and with the class. He began to feel persecuted. Evidently she had learned all she could from him in the writing of short stories for children and was now ready to profit from it, without thanks to him. She hinted that another, professional editor was interested in her work. She mentioned a commercial magazine that was corresponding with her. He had been used and he knew it. He grew bitter. His own work began to take on a new tone, violently disillusioned. In her presence, he would read from it slowly, oracularly, turning toward her as he read. The story would contain allusions to lost and betrayed hopes of love. No one in class missed the connection. Mrs. Cantwell sat listening gravely, during her last visit.

Bitterly Lawrence turned to ribald jokes upon himself and upon his lost love. He became frankly sexual and aggressive with other women. Fortunately for him the class atmosphere which he himself had encouraged lent itself to his conduct. None of the women whom he approached took offense, and none took him seriously either. He could make no progress with any of them, and the more obscene and coarse he became the less urgent grew his need to write. He lost all interest in the class itself. He lost all interest in writing. When he did finally collect enough money with which to mimeograph the next issues of his magazines, he did it rapidly and indifferently, without love or excitement. He felt he had done what was required of him, but others he knew had not, especially Mrs. Cantwell, who now symbolized that stern, hypocritical, uncharitable spirit with which he had always equated his father.

In what was nearly his last writing, Lawrence took up the subject of his father again. Writing in his late forties, approximately his father's age at the time of his birth,

Lawrence saw with overwhelming clarity the horror that had been wrought upon him by his father. It was no less than inhuman for a man to have blamed a newborn child for its mother's death and never to have spared that child those insane accusations. It was the act of a man obsessed with the evil in himself and seeing nothing but evil in others. Was it any wonder then that the son had fought all his life to free himself of this evil and proclaimed a kind of life that would be free of such destructiveness. He had gone to extremes in his fight against the extreme with which he had been confronted since childhood. He had been touched by a madness in seeking to free himself from his father's madness. This was all there was to say about himself, and it was not much. Knowing his own irrationality and what it had done to him, somehow he could sympathize with his father now and understand.

Because he had lost interest and could not show enthusiasm for anything, his class dwindled to a handful of devoted elderly women who doted on his eccentricities. Lawrence would talk at random about Joyce and Proust, although they meant little to him now. The class, at the end composed of only three genteel shabby women, was finally dissolved by the supervisor. Lawrence was returned to the relief rolls. It came as a blessing to him. He felt free again to go in search of his old friends and acquaintances in the Village.

But a search of the old haunts found everything changed. The old crowd had moved on. Friends had died, or were too old and weak to appear in public. The Village was full of strangers, young people recently out of college but with no knowledge of Lawrence or of his early struggles for academic freedom, and who ignored the old man, grey-haired, stoop-shouldered, stout, as he wandered among them with his arms full of bundles.

Lawrence was now thoroughly depressed. He spent his time at the movies, going to as many as three in one day. He would fall asleep in his seat, snoring through several hours of westerns and detective thrillers in the vacant movie houses of the Bowery.

One day his relief investigator came to visit him in the apartment that was still maintained for him in the vicinity of what had been Mrs. Cantwell's residence. He found Lawrence's manuscripts heaped like rubbish on the floor, in the leather chair and on the bed. He saw that, although Lawrence had slept on the floor in order not to disturb the arrangement of the papers, the manuscripts were thick with dust and had not been moved or touched for a long time. The investigator felt forced to describe Lawrence as senile. Nor did Lawrence have the spirit to oppose this judgment; in the presence of the investigator a dreary hysteria and incoherence would possess him, and the official was confirmed in his analysis. He concluded that Lawrence would not need an expensive apartment. It would only be necessary to dispose of the papers, and of the books and phonograph records and the battered rusted typewriter that also stood on the floor gathering dust. Unused and obviously ignored, all this "junk" could be disposed of in the garbage can, and the apartment made available for a full family, while Lawrence could spend the rest of his years in a hall bedroom in one of the cheap tenements off the Bowery.

Lawrence C. Woodman was born in Barrington, New Hampshire on June 2, 1890. He entered Bates College in the fall of 1910 and graduated in 1914. He studied at Columbia University, mostly during summer sessions, between 1919 and 1923. He gave up or was dismissed from his teaching position at Coe College in 1928. He lives now in New York City, where he is active as a painter, in the same kind of penury that Mr. Ignatow describes in this account of his earlier life. [Editor's note. Woodman died in 1965.]

1965

Unfinished Business

In 1937 I edited the literary magazine *Analytic.* Earlier I
had been associated with the short-lived *Literary Arts,
American Scene,* and *Womankind,* all three headed by
that amazing eccentric, Lawrence C. Woodman. One rea-
son for the failure of all three was a lack of money, com-
plicated by Woodman's bizarre impracticality. He had
insisted on issuing them simultaneously, on a survival
income from a WPA teaching job which also had to sup-
port his wife, daughter, and himself. Woodman was
driven by idealistic Herculean ambition which unfortu-
nately went to prove his inability to realize it, but he
had hold of a truth about our literary condition which
only in a scattered, desultory way was being acknowl-
edged and discussed by others. Despite my misgivings as
to the practical outcome of his extravagant scheme, I
helped in every way I could to publish his three periodi-
cals and to have them distributed widely. It was several
years before the second number of *American Scene* ap-
peared, the other two coming out each spaced about six
months apart, after which there was silence over them
all. In the meanwhile I had had invaluable contact direct
and indirect with writers from all over the country, get-
ting their views of Woodman's ideas and their own reflec-
tions on life and current literature in this country. This

gave me the opportunity to form my own theories. Vague through they were, they grew out of a difficult literary and personal position.

Woodman, whose magazines are listed and described in the Hoffman-Allen-Ulrich the *Little Magazine,* was strongly opposed to the bland, pragmatic-transcendental pap published regularly then in the *Atlantic, Harper's,* and other magazines. He could praise such magazines as the *Anvil* and the *New Masses* for their emphasis on the poverty and neglect being endured by the workers and farmers, but he condemned their prose and poetry as self-defeating because of the absence of individuality, the neglect of characterization and the general slighting of an American tone that could give the writing authenticity. As for the more representative national magazines, while he found in their stories and poems a sense of place, the language and characterizations were employed to gloss over essentially superficial insights. In his magazines Woodman hoped to bridge the gap between the two most important trends in American writing at this time. He wanted from the *Anvil* and the *New Masses* angry concern with the economic plight and isolation of the American worker and farmer, and from the more urbane magazines, such as the *Atlantic,* their sense of style. This project was to be fulfilled by his magazine the *American Scene.* In the *Literary Arts,* the emphasis was to be on psychological insight and on highly experimental style. Woodman was an enthusiastic follower of James Joyce and Gertrude Stein.

Needless to say, however, during the 1930s the will to experiment with techniques was not nearly as strong among American writers as was their immediate need to tell their truth with what methods they had at hand. They were being oppressed by their own acutely insecure economic and social position in a depressed society and had little or no disposition to probe for style or subtlety. Certainly a lack of money and the innate impracticality of Woodman were two causes for the eventual silence of his three magazines, but contributing in a decisive way to their early deaths was the limited response from writers and readers. The literary world of the 1930s was sharply divided between the so-called proletarian school and the complex of polite literature represented by the *Atlantic,* the *Saturday Evening Post,* the *American Mercury, Harper's,* and the many women-oriented magazines. The vast majority of writers and readers went one way or the other. In *Womankind,* the third of Woodman's magazines to fail after a second issue, there was an attempt to combine the elements of experimentation and sociological observation, with only women as contributors. The response from readers was even less than for the *American Scene* and the *Literary Arts.*

Woodman, however, in a last flare-up of enthusiasm proposed that I edit my own magazine, following my own ideas. Whatever spare money he had left over from his unsuccessful ventures, together with the meager receipts from sales would go towards subsidizing the first issue of *Analytic.* Like Woodman, I too had to condemn both literary camps for their mediocre productions, but my explanation and my solution for this failure differed basically from Woodman's. In his view, there were two groups, spiritually and ideologically divided. In my view, they were simply two sides of the same coin. Was not Albert Halper being printed in *Harper's* and the *Menorah Journal,* to mention just two respectable publications? Recently, his first novel, *Union Square,* a book written out of sympathy with the Communists, had been published by Viking. Halper wrote sadly and even gently, if sentimentally, of privation and class struggle. His writing never shouted. There were few exclamation points in his description of victory or defeat in the class-struggle May Day parades. His stories for national magazines were even more muted, with close, loving attention to individual lives in private circumstances. He was well-suited to present the Marxist position in a middle-class milieu. In fact, his work was indistinguishable from the great majority of stories published in *Harper's* and such magazines; descriptions of characters and situations hardly differed from those of the more folksy kind of writer favored by these middle-class publications. In all the prose, poetry, and short stories published between the two supposedly hostile camps, I could find only a difference of tone. Both sides made man out to be a product of society. But what was society? To the Marxists, shouting at the tops of their lungs, society was explained by their theory of labor value in any given environment. Man was the sum of his worth in the labor market. A laborer was worth almost nothing, because he could be hired cheaply. An executive, or an owner of a business, or a hired professional was a key figure because of the income he could command, consequently because of the power he enjoyed. The theory turned on money. Man and money formed an equation, man evaluated according to the amounts of money he possessed or could control.

To the liberals, the polite magazine crowd, this thinking was implicit, with, however, a touching regard for the quality of one's response as a person. In other words, it was okay to live by the buck, so long as one knew about it. That somehow kept you free. All this was beside the point for me. I saw that neither side had any conception of or insight into the restlessness that was gripping the country, in strikes and mass migrations. Class differences and class war were not at the heart of it. Neither was it a concern with economics, as put forward in the Communist or more moderate view. It was no longer money for its own sake, either. That was in the past, when all those amenities deriving from money had ruled their lives and marked success or failure. It was something that had grown on them, following the initial shock of the failure and near bankruptcy of the country's economic life. It certainly was not reflected in the stories they read in popular magazines for "entertainment." It had to be discovered by talking with them directly, living among them, sounding them out, making friends of them in their lonely hours. I had that opportunity in many a sleazy office job during working hours, lunch hours, and on the way home in crowded subways. I had the opportunity in the squalid neighborhoods in which I was forced to live and when visiting among relatives living on tree-lined and garden-bordered streets. The response always was the same. People were deeply pessimistic.

With money they had hoped to keep the path of life straight and smooth. But when money gives out, what then? With what did one build a path straight and smooth then? It was not only the striving for money that was in question but all that money brought with it, power, prestige, status. If all this could be wiped out in one day, as the crash had just taught, what then did man exist for? There was emptiness, and this was the heart of the problem facing everyone, and neither the Marxists nor the American pragmatic economists, thinkers and humanist writers were prepared or willing to deal with this question. The people were rejecting all the values and panaceas of the market.

My contact with numerous writers from all parts of the country, as I worked with Woodman and when shaping my own magazine, supported me in this observation. Robert Traver from the midwest, Cornel DeJong in New England, Harry Brown in the east, Alfred Morang the writer and traveling musician, Langston Hughes, Kerker Quinn, Weldon Kees, Forest Anderson, Millen Brand, and many others outside the influence of either literary grouping. I was receiving letters and manuscripts from men and women who were deep in the life of their country as husbands, fathers, wives, working for a living, raising families, trying to write after hours or doing free-lance work or simply looking for work while on relief. The common strain through their letters was a bitterness with existence as it was, not from an inability to make ends meet but from a questioning of a way of life in which everything depended finally on money for existence, even the very things by which one took delight in life. Of necessity, it even entered into one's way of thinking about oneself, and that was poisonous. It filled everyone with dangerous despair. In my magazine, I tried to publish as much of this material as I could get. I wanted the person to be seen as he really felt and lived in this period, and I wanted to show this person deep in his effort to rescue something of inalienable good, utterly divorced from those standards which a respect for money imposed. It had to be something in which he could root his dignity and self-respect without fear of losing either in the market shuffle.

At this time scores of magazines were springing up to bring the cruel situation of want and personal deprivation to the minds and souls of the American people. Many of these mimeographed or hand set magazines were being subsidized out of the Home Relief pennies of men and women determined to see that their case was put before the world. These crudely printed issues were the training ground for some of the finest writers of today. And now in the 1960s suddenly it is as if the 1930s were coming to life again in all their passion and anger. I can only refer to the New York scene, but I do imagine it corresponds to what is happening all over the country. In New York we now have on the stands a protest magazine called *Umbra,* edited jointly by Negroes and whites, with the one theme of the violation of the Negro race. In its second number, it already has brought forward Negro poets important for the freedom with which they speak of the sickness of a nation that can tolerate the willful degradation of even a single human being. The poetry and short stories are by no means perfect, but the voices are authentic, as in the 1930s, and they will be heard and have a bearing upon the fate of the country. The excitement is there. I foresee a major change in the life and literature of our times.

1965

Accents of Death and Endurance

"Kaddish," the poem from which the title of Allen Ginsberg's book is taken (*Kaddish and Other Poems 1958-1960*), can only be read with compassion, tears, inward graveling sobs, and terror and destruction in one's bones. The poem fixes upon the reader a mask of death through which he feels his very being disintegrating.

A family is exploded through the insanity of the mother. Nothing is left; there is only the sound of raving and mad acts. The youngest son is a child. He brings his mother to an institution and he is left to go home alone. Thus the poet begins his creative life.

Years later he commemorates her death in an asylum and his birth as a poet in accents of death, destruction, and despair, sweeping his entire world into the poem. It is a very recognizable world, with houses, streets, bedrooms, kitchens, food, poverty, ideals, and ambitions, all distorted in the face of a mad mother and issuing in the frightful voice of her son as poet. And as this world lives, it grabs by the hair. The reader must go insane, be destroyed with the mother, and resurrected in the poet who saves him in a whisper of holiness and dependence on God, to the sound of "Caw caw caw Lord Lord Lord caw caw caw Lord."

Only the holy may turn their backs on "Kaddish," for they are facing God, their backs made straight. This is a poem coarse and crying, wicked and pitiful, at the point before a man cracks. Slowly, in inflections blasphemous and obscene, always frightened and enraged, the poem turns to God, and help comes.

All this may seem astounding to say about a poet who has been tagged as the most outrageous of the beats, but there it is on the page to be read by anyone. "Kaddish" is a confession of the criminal in one's life. It is an act of purification, an expression of the need to be accepted, understood, and loved. It succeeds, not by any rule of religion or poetics, but simply because it has form and mass and drives forward into the day. This poem, I believe, will be read many years from now as one of the great modern acts of faith, rising classically out of the extremes of human life.

The rest of Ginsberg's slim book is anticlimactic. There are profoundly shocking, tragic things said in "Magic Psalm" and elsewhere, but it is only in "Kaddish" that Ginsberg achieves a major breakthrough of the spirit into open life, committing himself as he is, as he must suffer himself, into the hands of others, for good or evil. From "Kaddish," part one:

> Nameless, One Faced, Forever beyond me, beginningless, endless, Father in death. Tho I am not there for this
>   Prophecy,
> I am unmarried, I'm hymnless, I'm Heavenless, headless in blisshood I would still adore.

Ginsberg, if he must be critically evaluated, first must be approached as an integral being directed at a certain goal, much as Walt Whitman has been treated. The differences between them, despite certain similarities in style, are fundamental and diverse: Whitman discovers God everywhere, buoyantly, expansively reaching out with a caress, giving to life a final exultant mystery.

Ginsberg is hammerlike, smashing away until nothing is left but the great unsmashable dark void that yet clangs and stays intact and, under tremendous blows, forms an anthem in praise of God.

As a religious contemporary of Ginsberg, Harvey Shapiro is a remarkable contrast. Both are Jews and both draw on Hebraic sources, yet the differences are astounding. Shapiro apparently has had thorough academic training and is a scholar in his poetic interests. His tone often is ruminant, putting one in mind of his acknowledged rabbinical masters. The language is precise yet flowing, the images drawn from history. The vision is penetrant. A studied, controlled calm pervades the whole.

To go from Allen Ginsberg to Harvey Shapiro is an exercise in poetic gymnastics, from powerful rough and tumble to the loping stride of the long distance runner. It is idle to choose between them. The point is that from widely divergent sections of our society two very different poets converge upon the fear, mystery, and worship of their one God. Here is Shapiro in a poem called "The Book" (from *Mountain, Fire, Thornbush*):

> Violent in its blood, the dark book
> Hangs like a tree of night upon the sky.
> It batters history, that genesis,
> Word that whelped a world up,
> While priest and king and all
> Raged at the syntax they were swaddled by.
>
> And this is law, or so is said
> Within the darkening synagogue
> By old men, honored in their beards
> By the unsealed, heroic sounds.
> Celebration without end, the dark book
> Whispers to the wind,
> Wind cradles the destructive globe.

Outside, the night is far away.
Space is empty. One might touch,
If the necessary power were given,
All with human eloquence.
What hangs upon the tree is man.
With his blood the book is written.

Shapiro's poems are as significant as Ginsberg's be-
cause of their very objectivity, intellectual detachment,
and skepticism. He has built a style characteristic of his
thinking which still retains highly sensitive antennae to
all that goes on within and without. It is "sensitive" be-
cause it reminds both the reader and the poet that objec-
tivity and detachment generally are but a way of steeling
oneself to the chaos within and without.

One is helpless to end the chaos in either case, but if
God's will is a civilizing one, then it must be expressed
as a kind of grace before evil, a grace which, while carry-
ing every innuendo of violence and depravity, can yet
retain an attachment to order by its accent, its detach-
ment. This is the essence of Shapiro's intellectual and
poetic creed. It is a superb capstone to Ginsberg's horror
and ecstasy.

I want to commend particularly Shapiro's realistic
lyricism in "Death of a Grandmother," one of the finest
deliverances of grief-and-love ambivalence it has been
my joy to read. This poet has trained himself for the
long stretch, he knows what there is to know and has
girded himself accordingly. His poems are—in his own
phrase from "Spirit of Rabbi Nachman"—"Words mov-
ing a bit of air / So that the whole morning moves."
From Harvey Shapiro we may look forward to verse of
quintessent comfort and endurance.

1961

The Past Reordered

I am moved by a sense of purification in this book (Harvey Shapiro, *Battle Report*). *Battle Report* consists of selections from three previous collections and an opening group of more recent poems, an arrangement which impels the reader to seek out certain implications. Here is a poem, "Past Time," from the late period:

> I believe we came together
> Out of ignorance not love,
> Both being shy and hunted in the city.
> In the hot summer, touching each other,
> Amazed at how love could come
> Like a waterfall, with frightening force
> And bruising sleep. Waking at noon,
> Touching each other for direction,
> Out of ignorance not love.

And here is "The Marriage," from *Mountain, Fire, Thornbush,* Harvey Shapiro's third book, published in 1961:

> When they were canopied, and had the wine
> To lace their spirits in the trembling cup,
> And all the holy words sang round their heads
> In tribute to the maker and the vine,
> He saw the leeching sea lap, like darkness,

Up her summer's gown, as if dark time
And he should race to claim the maidenhead.
When he smashed the cup, then ruin spread.
The dazzled floor showed sea and blood.
Beyond this harvest that the ritual bore
(Their mothers weeping on the farther shore)
They saw the journeying years extend.
And Zion's hill rose for their reckoning.

Consider in the latter the conception of the dark, sacramental wine likened to death as at the same time it draws the marriage into direct relationship with the eternal godhead. Bride and bridegroom, journeying toward Zion, the manifest eternal, are fixed forever in their relationship toward each other, removed from the exigencies of a transient world. Acting in support, the ritual language lifts the wedding to its symbolical level of absolute truth, to the measure of the traditional and majestical iambic foot, rhymed.

Then examine the language of "Past Time" in its very nearly brutal gesture. Direct, plain, matter of fact in tone, without flourish or apology, it sets the marriage in its ordinary, quotidian, circumstantial text. God, Zion, and preordination are either abolished or, having vanished in the daily struggle for existence, are now forgotten without regret or afterthought. A fury of discovery races through the poem to give it the curt power of its accomplishment. We are alone and that is the point Harvey Shapiro hammers home in the language and in the text, alone with no one but ourselves to preside over our faults, frailties, the world being just this, ours to make.

All these recent poems, including "Past Time," could be grouped together as one, with the effect of each leading to the next. Uncompromising in tone and point of view, their content would permit conjecture as to what precisely in the poet's life led to such a radical change of style. But that would be irrelevant to the point of the poems, which is that they are entirely a fresh departure, written with a vigor altogether different from and even superior to the earlier poems. They spring from a dual vision in the poet of disillusionment, and regeneration born from disillusionment. That which led to his despair turns out not to have had basis in reality in the first place, its connection with reality specious at most. The permanent and immutable are to be found in the processes of life itself, of which we are one expression, no matter what form of it we take. To live is to endure and it is through endurance that we manifest the energy of life:

> I cast out
> Beyond the demonic element
> And the fear of death
> (And the fear of death)
> Into that bright water
> Beyond this water
> Where leviathan swims.
> Communication is instant
> When it comes—close
> As my hand, the words on my tongue,
> Though the crying in my ear
> Is my own death crying.

Harvey Shapiro has been able to extend this achievement into the public area of our lives, to give us one of the few notable poems on the death of President Kennedy, "National Cold Storage Company":

> The National Cold Storage Company contains
> More things than you can dream of.
> Hard by the Brooklyn Bridge it stands
> In a litter of freight cars,
> Tugs to one side; the other, the traffic
> Of the Long Island Expressway.

I myself have dropped into it in seven years
Midnight tossings, plans for escape, the shakes.
Add to this the national total—
Grant's tomb, the Civil War, Arlington,
The young President dead.
Above the warehouse and beneath the stars
The poets creep on the harp of the Bridge.
But see,
They fall into the National Cold Storage Company
One by one. The wind off the river is too cold,
Or the times too rough, or the Bridge
Is not a harp at all. Or maybe
A montrous birth inside the warehouse
Must be fed by everything—ships, poems,
Stars, all the years of our lives.

The poignancy of this poem has also its application to the many recent poems of love and marriage in the book. These are not written from defeat either but out of a need to know if one would live.

Despite the contrast the earlier work makes with the new poems, it is very much a preparation for what follows. I am referring especially to Shapiro's experience as an Air Force radio gunner in World War II, used in an account in retrospect in the title poem to the book, "Battle Report." Too long to quote in full, the poem is clearly written out of an obsession with the experience:

In this slow dream's rehearsal,
Again I am the death-instructed kid,
Gun in its cradle, sun at my back,
Cities below me without sound.
That tensed, corrugated hose
Feeding to my face the air of substance,
I face the mirroring past.
We swarm the skies, determined armies,
To seek the war's end, the silence stealing,
The mind grown hesitant as breath.

Defeated in his effort at a relatively calm redress, Shapiro continued to search still further back in his past for other ways to recover himself. With his exceptional knowledge of Hebrew history and religion, such poems as "The Wedding" followed, rich in evocation of Hebrew faith and wisdom, and poignant with his need. From "Dream of Life":

> But yesterday I saw
> Seven gulls pass overhead.
> It may be tonight I will dream myself
> Into a promise of life.

In his way, Shapiro repeats the experience of countless young men after the war in search of a surety of some kind that life comes first, after all. Many did finally manage to come to terms with their past of bomb and bayonet and to lead a fairly normal existence, digging as far as they could without loss of self-respect into ritual and the secular conformations of America. These became for them their haven, allowing them to live contentedly (or perhaps not so contentedly) for the balance of their days with wives, children, mortgaged homes, television sets, and cars: the evidence of a fulfilled existence. In Harvey Shapiro another thing was at work. The after-strain of war, it could be said, continued to act on him, with this latest book as a result, in which he decisively sheds the religious aura and again as in his gunner days stands exposed—but shield and weapon are himself now, invulnerable in his life. In "News of the World":

> The past, like so many bad poems,
> Waits to be reordered,
> And the future needs reordering too.
> Rain dampens the brick,
> And the house sends up its smell
> Of smoke and lives—

My own funk the major part.
Angling for direction,
I think of the favored in Homer,
Who in a dream, a council meeting,
At the bottom of despair,
Heard the voice of a god or goddess,
Though it was, say, only Polites
Speaking. Turning to a friend,
I ask again
For news of the world.

1967

Poet of the City

Of Being Numerous is George Oppen's fourth book of poetry and his best. The title poem gathers up his major themes into a single vision: man in his city, the city as an expression of man at a given time that is now. For those who have read William Carlos Williams's *Paterson,* one of the great modern American epics, *Of Being Numerous* will have striking parallels.

Both Williams and Oppen concentrate upon the anonymity and incoherence of city life. They see the crowd and its mass movement through the streets as a futile, wasted energy in which the uniqueness of the individual, as Oppen has it, is obliterated by the sheer weight and density of numbers.

For these poets, communication no longer exists between persons, for the sense of self, that strength and stability that could support enduring personal relationships, has been shattered. In the flux of city life, often wrenching and violent, the individual is subjected to the pressure for perpetual change simply to survive, only to become unrecognizable even to himself. The tragedy is compounded as people become anonymous to one another and form the mass. It is at this point, however, that the two poets diverge significantly in their solutions to the problems raised.

Williams resolves them in the symbol of traditional aesthetic content. I am referring to book five of *Paterson* with its central image of the unicorn as sexual, life enhancing, therefore free to do its own will (though book six, still in the note taking stage at Williams's death, was already beginning to abandon that image as essentially limited in its relation to the complex, impersonal city). Oppen, in the poem "Of Being Numerous," finds his solution by determining to remain exposed to the city. Amid the aimless rush and noise of his environment, he means to function as a person upon that seedless asphalt bed where he was born.

The difference resides in the conception of the poet's role in reacting to the kind of crisis the city represents. Williams would set the man apart who can form a way independent of the disparate, disorganized, unformed elements that are the city. For Oppen, no man can divorce himself from the crisis to lead his own unique existence. Once he understands and accepts his own involvement with this crisis, however, he may rescue the self through the consistent exercise of consciousness, which is the self in being. And since that is the desired result of the use of consciousness, it is to Oppen a successful exercise:

> Because the known and the unknown
> Touch,
>
> One witnesses—
> It is ennobling
> If one thinks so.
>
> If to know is noble
> It is ennobling.

These are the words of a man determined to live with or without the shield of his aesthetic sensibility, for the crisis has eclipsed that possibility and must be faced and lived with in all its ugliness and threat to life itself. Paradoxically, it is this intense participation in, and grappling with, chaos that forges the title poem. Its very sound, movement, and the frequent first person standpoint—elliptical and muted like a man bending before a storm—draws us into his struggle to survive:

> We are pressed, pressed on each other,
> We will be told at once
> Of anything that happens
>
> And the discovery of fact bursts
> In a paroxysm of emotion
> Now as always. Crusoe
>
> We say was
> 'Rescued.'
> So we have chosen

These lines point up the important difference between the two poets in their view of the city. As a doctor practicing in the slums of Passaic, New Jersey, Williams was able to associate empathetically with the men and women trapped in that life. He could experience their spiritual incoherence and fragmentation, finally to project it as the metaphor of being itself in this country.

Williams was profoundly sensitive, but he felt himself to be ultimately independent of his environment. He could characterize the situation objectively through a large number of dispersed images, such as the park preacher, the various letter writers, Mr. Paterson, the Giant (waterfalls), the poet, the doctor, and so on. Williams was a multiple of juxtaposed voices, dramatizing his despair of communitas, even for himself. Oppen's

is the voice in which all is held in tension, there being no
choice for him, a man of the city:

> 'Whether as the intensity of seeing
> increases, one's distance
> from Them, the people does
> not also increase'
>
> I know, of course I know, I can
> enter no other place
>
> Yet I am one of those who from
> nothing but man's way of
> thought and one of his dialects
> and what has happened
> to me
>
> Have made poetry.

What is so remarkable here is that Oppen has been
able to resolve the very pressures of disintegration in the
writing of such a deeply integrated poem. It becomes an
exhilarating exhibition of strength in complexity that
one is drawn to with enthusiasm and hope.

Technically, the title poem is divided into thirty-nine
brief sections, each virtually a poem in itself but related
through subject and, primarily, by a transitional mode
of writing. The poet progresses from self-doubt and self-
searching through the artifacts of the city, to a moment
in which his mind is revealed to itself as its own strength:

> Tho the world
> Is the obvious, the seen
> And unforseeable,
> That which one cannot
> Not see

Which the first eyes
Saw—

For us
Also each
Man or woman
Near is
Knowledge

Tho it may be of the moon's
Own vacuity

—and the mad, too, speak only
of conspiracy
and people talking—

And if those paths
Of the mind
Cannot break

It is not the wild glare
Of the world even that one dies in.

Stylistically, "Of Being Numerous" goes far beyond Oppen's earlier works in the power evoked through condensation and ellipsis. It is now a shorthand of the poetic act, with masterly strokes to underline meaning. If the city is the expression of man, then Oppen's poem surely is its finest exponent, in its capacity to think and to take pride in its judgments. A civilized poem, a lone being, it's true, but one for which we may feel ourselves fortunate. A comfort among the ashes.

The rest of the book consists of six relatively short poems. "Route" is the longest of the six and treats the identical theme taken up in "Of Being Numerous," but from the standpoint of love in its public and historical manifestations. I write "love" advisedly, for the subject undergoes bitter, resigned treatment in Oppen's hands:

Not the desire for approval nor
    even for love—O
that trap! From which escaped,
    barely—if it fails

We will produce no sane man
    again. . . .

. . . .

Nothing more real than boredom—
    dreamlessness, the
        experience of time, never felt
        by the new arrival,
        never at the doors, the thresh-
        olds, it is the native

Native in native time. . . .

The language, like that of the title poem, is terse,
aphoristic, or realistic by turns, from section to section.
"Route" could be set beside "Of Being Numerous" as a
powerful commentary upon the main subject matter in
that poem: as in "Of Being Numerous," the intelligence
and clarity, or consciousness, with which one views one-
self and one's times prevails to form a triumph of its
own.

In this respect, the entire book is of a piece. It is the
work of a man who rests his faith in the mind as a value
in itself on which the individual may depend. Concur-
rently, there is an awareness of disaster and chaos, this
awareness being an affirmation of the possibility of order.
Oppen is in the line of our best contemporary poets:
Wallace Stevens, William Carlos Williams, T. S. Eliot,
and Ezra Pound—carrying the point a step beyond them
in time, close to our very skin.

1968

245

Puritan Paradox

In his eighth volume of poetry, *Notebook 1967-68,*
Robert Lowell has returned to the iambic pentameter of
his earlier books, *Lord Weary's Castle* (1946) and *The
Mills of the Kavanaughs* (1951)—but with a pronounced
difference. Using the fourteen-line sonnet form, un-
rhymed, he attempts to adapt his tone to the level of
worldly, circumstantial affairs. This is clearly with the
intention of capturing and fixing, each in its own singu-
larity, the evanescent events and emotions that composed
his life, and the lives of his friends, relatives, and the
world around him, from day to day throughout the
course of one year.

The sonnet, in its concentration on a single insight or
metaphor, is certainly suited to the purpose. The infor-
mal approach that Lowell adopts, however, is obviously
in contradistinction to the apocalyptic, transcendent
anger of, say, "As a Plane Tree by the Water," in *Lord
Weary's Castle,* which is typical of his major style. His
new low-key treatment of materials familiar to readers
of his past work suggests a discovered, welcome desire
to meet the flux and drift of both the world and himself
on their own terms. Surely, this represents a triumph
of personal adjustment for the poet, who for years has
lived in agonizing confrontation with problems of the
spirit. Thus in "Dalliance," he ponders his past and pres-

ent conditions, achieving a tentative yet encouraging resolution in the last two lines:

> All was respectability, dark and secret,
> dalliance means to dwell the hours of Eros—
> this flower I take away and wear with fear;
> who ever noticed? Othello never caught
> Cassio reeking Desdemona's musk.
> You grow more comforting, as you excite;
> like the Macbeth murk of Manhattan in sunset smog.
> Is it a hobby like heroin or birds?
> Set at the helm, facing a pot of coals,
> the sleet and wind spinning me ninety degrees,
> I must not give me up then to the fire,
> lest it invert my fire; it blinded me;
> so did it me; there's wisdom that is woe,
> but there is a woe that is madness.

Elsewhere in the book, the anger and contempt aroused in him by the Democratic National Convention in Chicago, as well as certain tender poems to his daughter and wife, are further lightenings of Lowell's burden. Still, *Notebook 1967-68* as a whole (he would like us to view it as one poem) reflects his continued preoccupation with guilt and renunciation, and the predestined doom of hope or action. This is expressed with fullness in "Mexico":

> The difficulties, the impossibilities,
> stand out: I, fifty, humbled with the years' gold
> garbage,
> dead laurel grizzling my back like spines of hay;
> you, some sweet, uncertain age, say twenty-seven,
> unballasted by honor or deception.
> What help then? Not the sun, the scarlet blossom,
> and the high fever of this seventh day,
> the wayfarer's predestined diarrhea, nausea,
> the multiple mosquito spots, round as pesos.
> Hope not in God here, nor the Aztec gods;

we sun-people know the sun, the source of life,
will die, unless we feed it human blood—
we two are clocks, and only count in time;
the hand's knife-edge is pressed against the future.

I can imagine this sort of poem being written by
Lowell's cultural ancestor, the early Puritan poet Edward
Taylor, with his paradoxical and insatiable curiosity
about the world; he would have enjoyed the sensation
of mingling pleasure and exotic horror. True, Lowell is
not a throwback to the past. History, his own above all,
has taught him a skepticism toward his origins that we
can recall from earlier poems—"Dunbarton" and "At
the Indian Killer's Grave," among others. He still relies,
though, on the rhetorical posture of the Puritan faith—as
in the poem just quoted—and the reader therefore con-
tinues to see in his work a personal and world outlook
that by and large no longer obtains.

Puritan Calvinism, while often transmuted into con-
temporary and generally unrecognizable forms, remains
at the root of American experience. Hence, it is not sur-
prising that Lowell, a direct New England descendant,
should find himself living and writing in its context. But
to maintain his identity in this tradition of elect indi-
viduality represents a severe contradiction, since he is
painfully aware of the impersonal, undifferentiated char-
acter of the modern world. For all significant purposes,
his faith has lost its original relevance in the face of the
constant, almost automatic transformation each of us
undergoes every day. It is to this phenomenon that
Lowell would adapt himself by the use of his conversa-
tional tone, in an apparent search for a restatement of
his heritage in current terms. The language of some of
the new poems—"Sounds in the Night," for one—is al-
tered to accommodate an emphasis on the circumstan-

tial. Nevertheless, it echoes old disillusionment and moral presuppositions:

> Nothing new in them yet their old roles startle;
> asked to adapt, they swear they cannot swerve:
> machines our only friends who live to serve us,
> metal, mortal and mechanical,
> their dissonance varied as our northern birds—
> clean and singing through the night air dirt!
> Sleepless I drink their love, if it is love.
> Miles below heaven, luminous in some courtyard,
> dungeoned by wall-brick windowless,
> the grass conservative cry of the cat in heat—
> "Who cares if the running stream is sometimes stopped?
> Inexhaustible the springs from which I flow."
> Cats will be here when man is prehistory,
> man doomed to outlast the body of his work.

The style recalls the "free verse" line in *For the Union Dead* and *Life Studies,* and the poem itself succeeds in grasping the environment through its images. Yet the informal tone, an effort at a pragmatic approach, serves in the end merely to state past responses in a diluted form. Toward life's everyday particulars—which Lowell over and over has shown himself capable of handling vividly—he here remains, strangely enough, resigned and withdrawn. The poem lies flat on the page.

The conversational voice in "Sounds in the Night" is filled with that sense of futility we bring to our daily existence once we have reduced ourselves to insignificance in our own sight by comparison with the great, stony outside. Kept within itself, with reference only to preconceived ideas of order, such self-pity results in the destruction of the very objective for which it is supposed to exist: individuality and independence.

In poetry, a failure of this kind could derive from an

attempt to mediate between the "real" world and one-self without troubling too deeply with the effort. The method founders in ordinariness. Lowell's voice can be heard in these new poems—it could never be mistaken for another—but at a level that I suspect he may not have anticipated in using this mode of casual statement.

Accommodations, then, can be cited as the cause of the difficulties—*Notebook 1967-68* as a whole suffers from the defects of compromise. Lowell is not ready to give up that Puritan sense of things in which he was raised, or at least to modify it significantly for modern life. I stress this aspect of his influences in full awareness of his conversion to Catholicism many years ago. For it is his Puritan ethic, with its emphasis on the hopeless corruption of the spirit and doom without salvation, that finally emerges in these new poems.

Lowell is keenly aware of this sensibility, precisely toward those very excitements and abrasions of daily existence that are the inspiration to his thought and writing. As many of the poems indicate, this is the paradox he recognizes in himself, and which he is apparently unwilling or unable to resolve or reorient.

Another view of *Notebook 1967-68* is suggested by Lowell's concluding prose statement, "Afterthought." He asks that the 300 sonnets be looked on as a single poem—a kind of daily record of oneself and the world throughout a year, from summer to summer. This idea in itself expresses a faith in the ability of life to serve us under all conditions. It may also be seen as an effort to discover a shape to one's thoughts and responses through the very passage and impact of time and events.

Thus the book could have meaning for us as a personal epic, like William Carlos Williams's *Paterson* and Ezra Pound's *Cantos*. Indeed, the very scope of the material the poet covers would seem to lend itself to such a reading. For Lowell, however, the "opportunist" method and inspiration by "impulse" obviate personal transformation as a controlling principle of composition.

Even if *Notebook 1967-68* does not achieve the unity Lowell intended, some of the sonnets do manage to meet the challenge of his low-key manner, particularly those, like "Fear in Chicago," dealing with subjects that take the poet out of himself:

> The little millionaire's place, sheen of the centuries;
> as my eye roved, everything freshly French;
> then I saw a score marked *sans rigueur*
> on the little grand piano, muddy white,
> a blank white and medallion-little bust
> of Franz Schubert, a blown-up colored photograph
> of the owner's wife, executive-Bronzino—
> this frantic touch of effort! Or out-window,
> two cunning cylinder skyscraper apartment buildings—
> six circles of car garage below the homes,
> moored boats below the cars—more Louis Quinze
> and right than anything in this apartment;
> except the little girl's bedroom, perfect with posters:
> "Do not enter," and "Sock it to me, Baby."

Equally effective are several portraits of poet friends, family poems, poems about historical figures, and a translation from Dante. For the most part, these too are limited by Lowell's reluctance to relate affirmatively to the outside world, even in tragic terms. But they are surely welcome, above all as possible hints at what is to come in future poems.

1969

James Wright

Shall We Gather at the River is James Wright's fourth book of poems and the most personal and affecting. To write of his work, early or late, is to indicate its personal quality, but with this book he reaches its pith. He has made it a metaphor of our land. Mr. Wright was born and raised in the Midwest, at its navel of blast furnaces and squalid shack towns where are born the advertised good things of our life and our position in the world.

The title of the book, taken from the revered old Methodist-Revivalist hymn, is put to the bitterest use in several of the river poems dealing with vagrants with whom the poet identifies. They stand or lie beside the banks of the chemically filthy Ohio River contemplating suicide by drowning to escape a blight worse than physical death. Like the ruined river, they are used up and nondescript to their contemporaries. To read these poems is to be brought to a mainstream of American consciousness:

> Under the enormous pier-shadow,
> Hobie Johnson drowned in a suckhole.
> I cannot even remember
> His obliterated face.
> Outside my window, now, Minneapolis
> Drowns, dark.

It is dark.
I have no life.

What is left of all of it?
Blind hoboes sell American flags
And bad poems of patriotism
On Saturday evenings forever in the rain,
Between the cathouses and the slag heaps
And the river, down home.
Oh Jesus Christ, the Czechoslovakians
Are drunk again, clambering
Down the sand-pitted walls
Of the grave.

This is the poetry of a man in control of his art and of these circumstances. If he has been trapped, as he feels himself to be, partly of his own doing—he can free himself only as Hobie Johnson does. James Wright has chosen to write of this directly and to expose himself in this condition for all to come to his rescue, if they are not lost in their own hobo spirit. Is America the land of vagrants, his anguish asks, where the many have learned to camouflage themselves in the better made suits, living in meticulously kept homes as a defense against the nothingness that grabs at them? Writing of it, Mr. Wright makes a place of it from which to speak. He triumphs in his despair.

It is the bitter price of all important art and Mr. Wright has paid in full:

Crouched down by a roadside windbreak
At the edge of the prairie,
I flinch under the baleful jangling of wind
Through the telephone wires, a wilderness of voices
Blown for a thousand miles, for a hundred years.
They all have the same name, and the name is lost.
So: it is not me, it is not my love
Alone lost.

The grief that I hear is my life somewhere.
Now I am speaking with the voice
Of a scarecrow that stands up
And suddenly turns into a bird.
This field is the beginning of my native land,
This place of skull where I hear myself weeping.

In another poem, he writes of the gentle resignation
of his father, a steel worker, who with calm patience
raised a family in some comfort. The poet on a home-
coming visit from his own ambitious intellectual and
professional striving finds at the meeting point between
them, as they sit together near a stove, a consuming emp-
tiness. His father has made the self-sacrifice demanded
in a society that cares nothing for the individual, in its
headlong corporate drive.

Mr. Wright is the heir of Theodore Dreiser, Sherwood
Anderson, and Edgar Lee Masters, men who pierced
through to the quality of American life, but a cause for
celebration now is the strength with which the poet sur-
vives beneath the steamroller America. A poet who can
write with the freshness of his grief has given himself
the joy of his identity.

Technically, Mr. Wright has taken several momentous
strides. By abandoning rhyme and its traditional forms in
virtually every poem, he has given himself the enormous
freedom of versatility and improvisation, precisely those
qualities required in a circumstance as dehumanizing as
the poems present.

At the same time, he has accomplished the rare and
exciting thing in American poetry today. He has made
an organic graft of the surrealist technique upon the
body of hard reality, one enhancing and reinforcing the
other so that we have a mode as evocative as a dream
and as effective as a newspaper account. It works with

fascinating, chanting power: "The stars / Have gone down. / What does my anguish / Matter? Something / The color / Of a puma has plunged through this net, and is gone."

1969

IV

Personal Prose

IV

Personal Prose

Apartment House Blues

There are petunias here. They are planted along a wall opposite my window. Looking down on them, I am amazed to find them there, considering it a miracle that the children have not by this time uprooted them and thrown them to the ground. Everywhere are children. They come pouring out of the apartments centered around the courtyard or come up from other buildings on the block. By early morning their cries and voices have risen to a steady roar, like the surf. One eventually learns to ignore it and go about one's thinking and work, but by that time one begins to wonder what in the world was the purpose in bringing so many children to life, when all they seem capable of is this steady roar. Mothers, sooner or later, stick their heads out the windows and add their screams of admonition or command. How much different, I wonder, is all this from the old-fashioned tenement dwellings from which we were supposed to have fled to these modern improvements? If any have been made, I would say it is in the increased volume of sound from what it was during the tenement regime. Now there is a grass courtyard around which the buildings are grouped and which acts as an amplifier. You can lock yourself in the clothes closet in the room farthest from this roar and still feel its pressure behind the door. It is then that one resigns oneself to the increasing birthrate and to the tendency among the young to marry and beget children, on whom they vent their spleen from windows.

They themselves are distracted and made unhappy by the noise and the constant need to attend the children in one way or another. I begin to look at the whole scheme of reproduction as a vast mistake. Come Saturday morning, the start of the weekend and relaxation, and the father is at home, howling for his rest and peace. The children are at home or his wife has begun to nag him to take the children off her hands. She has had them all week, steadily. Some husbands roar, others scream and choke. Some wives rattle away hysterically in reply or simply start to beat up the children, whose voices begin to blend with the sounds of their tormented parents.

Rent is higher here too than in tenements, now that hot water and steam heat are provided and janitor service assured. An incinerator stands behind a closed door in the hallway, ready to accept all and any rubbish and refuse. The apartment floors are parquet. There is more window area. In fact, one does not know which way to turn to dress or undress free of the stares of one's neighbors across the courtyard. During the winter, the window shades go up and down all day, and in summer stay up because the heat makes it unbearable to keep out the air even for a moment, and so one gets all one wants of bodies in all states of dress and undress, until the sight is sickening and a pall on one's sense of pleasure and mystery. One begins to wonder of what use it is to live, when one is robbed of so much of the ritual of everyday existence. Inward brooding and lassitude set in; one becomes introverted in the dullest manner, with a need for a soporific, anything that will soothe one's violent distaste for the surrounding life. One takes to reading the newspaper jokes, the headlines on rapes, gambling, communism, anything at all that will furnish diversion from the nakedness and unimaginativeness in which one is caught.

Women who at other times would present an attractive view to one's eye look woebegone and sloppy as they drag themselves about in their shorts or slips, mopping themselves of the heat and sweat in their apartments. The basic call to life becomes stunted in one and the next best thing seems to be a soda or an ice cream by which one may forget one's disillusion and sense of betrayal.

No, apartment houses of the modern kind, spacious and light, as advertised, are not the answer to living well, and the petunias that grow next to the wall in the court-yard seem as out of place here as a forest nymph would be in a coal yard.

When, I have begun to ask myself and to anticipate, will the children set to tearing out the falseness here of these flowers, for children are the barometer of the life being lived here. Already they have learned to attack one another with sticks and to tear huge clumps of grass and dirt out of the ground and hurl them at each other, in a kind of play in which they represent for one another the roles of crooks, cokies, gunmolls, and reds. During such intervals of peace and quiet as they occasionally ar-range among themselves, it is to plan new tactics for a fresh battle. They are not fools, these children. They learn the truth quickly and act upon it, living it with the sincerity and ruthlessness that grownups hardly dare at-tempt. The grownups, not daring to do so, offer as their excuse their efforts to compose some kind of peace and will to live among themselves and in themselves in har-mony. It is a laudable profession, but it is not reflected in the children, who pause from their make-believe mayhem only to rest and reorganize themselves for re-newed onslaughts, and when they are not at each other they are spending themselves in self-praise as fighters and shrewdies or in ridiculing these same abilities in their playmates.

I am of the opinion now that the reason those petunias stay untouched and unnoticed by the children is that they do not think these flowers worthy of their attention, and that to pull them out and fling them to the ground would be to express a dissatisfaction with the kind of lives they lead. I am convinced that instead of acting out their unhappiness with their lives they are indeed joyful at the opportunity to play in just this manner to which their lives lead them. Do they not come pouring out of their apartments each morning with pistols and sticks ready to give battle all over again after a night of sleep and dreaming of new violent strategies? Otherwise, why the bloom on their cheeks, the sturdiness of their bodies, the ring in their voices, the merriment with which they attack one another, and the pleasure with which they discuss their victories over each other; and what is this steady roar that rises from them but the expression of their energies at the highest level of fulfillment? They do what they enjoy, and if I am right in drawing this conclusion, then they have learned this from their parents too, who instead of suffering in their apartments are, in truth, making of this the prime experience of their lives, for which they would exchange none other. Certainly they have the television which absorbs them nightly with its review of the ghastly world news. They can sit apart and view the world as though they were not of it, and that what they experience every day as husband and wife is not what they are witnessing on the screen. This is the illusion they are given, so that looking on what is horrible and degrading, they can thank their stars that they have this margin of safety from which they may look on and think of their impassivity as their security and happiness.

In fantasy, I picture to myself the reaction of a family seated in front of their sets one evening. Suddenly it vanishes and in its place are live characters, the actual incident on their living room floor, the bloody, bandaged soldier sprawled on his face, the women and children lying in heaps, bones and gristle, one on top of the other, smoking stones and other such interesting events transpiring right in the room, so that if they would want to step to the kitchen refrigerator for the nightly soda or beer, they would have to climb over the bodies. But it is just possible that sitting in their living rooms and watching television they do feel sensitive to what they see. Looking down on the petunias, I think perhaps they are untouched all this while because they do mark for everyone in this courtyard some connection with life. The children do not touch the flowers perhaps because they sense it is their parents' wish for beauty, and theirs too, for that matter.

1950s

The Biggest Bomb

An Impressionistic Essay

It's best to write about things close to one's heart, if one wishes to write accurately. At the very least, the reader derives a sense of urgency and striving for honesty and understanding, even if, in the end, he finds he does not agree with the facts or interpretation of them. He knows, however, that he is being treated with respect as a person by a writer who desires as much in return. Between them they lay a basis for amity and peace, peace in its purest form, in which compassion decides everything.

I despair of myself. I walk around as with a hood over my head, to cloak my identity. Constantly I guard against lifting the hood to laugh. What am I hiding from, I ask, or closer yet, what needs to be shielded from me? Am I a menace in a land of abundant forests, great fertile plains, large calm lakes filled with fish—a country that needs simply to press buttons to feed and clothe itself and to pour its surplus into other hands that are tense with need? How am I a menace, I who simply walk the streets beneath the tallest buildings in the world, in the vicinity of the most powerful and liberal banks in history? I deal with words, I give myself the pleasure of being free with my feelings, my thoughts. I allow them to fall into any shape or color they desire in words. I surround myself with a world that is in my head and nowhere else, and that cannot take possession of anyone without the person's consent. According to our constitution, this is the pure freedom we desire for one another; but emerging from my house to step out into the street, I put my thoughts in order along a certain track that runs side by side with many other tracks and I become as a conductor of my own train, guarding against vagabonds, unpaid passengers, lateness, and unruly behavior on the train. I become a guardian of schedules, rules, and manners. I become my opposite.

Wherein am I a menace to cause distressed looks when I raise my hood or shout through it that I am smothering, that the world around me is mad for forcing me to wear a hood, unless I would risk my life? This feeling for freedom in my poems will make others forget themselves and start on a trail into a forest, as far from city life as possible, as far from the sound and suction of machines as woods can afford, but this is the warning I read in angry looks. My words will evaporate skyscrapers, banks, hotels, housing projects, parks, railroads, clinics for the poor, hospitals for the mentally ill. I am a menace to myself too is what the angry looks warn, since I too have need of skyscrapers, banks, housing projects, benefits of clinics, and hospitals for the mentally ill. Assuming I am ill, where then will I go for treatment? My words are risen from primeval darkness, trailing huge clouds of night with them to blanket the world with chaos. The freedom I write about is for cockroaches, ants, mice, and lice, who have no other life from birth and cannot change. They take their food where they find it, raise their families in shelters where they find them, in holes, cracks, corners, and drainpipes. My words are more dangerous than radioactive dust. Once read, they leave behind life shrunk to the misery of an insect existence. Better dead! Why then, I ask myself, am I allowed to live? I do not dare ask them, but I suspect that my hood is my sign of repentance, guilt, regret. In this condition I make the observer's life meaningful to him. Now he may enjoy his way with zest, free of the guilt which I have taken on myself, perversely. Hurry with the golf clubs, drag out the yacht, open up another bottle of bourbon, the monk is walking by, stifling and sad but who gives pleasure and relief to others with his burden.

So my words, my poems are poisonous and they have poisoned me, with a wish for freedom to speak, to dance, to raise my arms. I am the quintessence of all that is wrong with the natural man. He will not conform to standards, he will not ride the subway with pleasure, he will not sit himself down at a desk in an office with relish, nor take his place at a machine with delight. He arrives at work sorrowfully, he removes his coat slowly, reluctantly, and he complains all day of the conditions and the pay. Toward the end of the working day, he speeds up his activities in order to be finished on time, so that he may hurry home at once to stuff himself with food before he is tempted to dope or drink. Seated in front of his television set, he is unhappy, nothing there on the screen offers him a way out, everything is in praise of things as they are. And they will improve, chortles the advertisement. "Crispy Crunch" will be even more crispy and crunchy next year! Go to bed, despair whispers. Sleep, bury yourself in dreams, in forgetfulness. While the body beside him, that of his wife, is filled too with the languor of his misery. Her body presses up against his for release, but no release can come. Tomorrow she must continue to raise her children in the same conditions as yesterday. But it is criminal to feel this way. It is a threat against the general welfare, it undermines one's confidence in the future, at a time such as this, threatened by atomic havoc from without. He must keep in step, he must set still higher standards of production for himself to avoid disaster. He does want to live, but is it possible this atomic bomb might end for all time production norms? This is criminal thinking of the lowest kind.

Yes, this poet is a menace with his wish for freedom and a need to stretch his arms. He will be obliterated. He has been forced to marry and to raise children, he has been condemned to buying a house in the suburbs, to taking on a large mortgage, to catching his train each morning *on time,* and to relaxing in his garden weekends with a spade and rake, so that he sits down with a deep sigh in front of his television set and welcomes with glazed eyes the torpidity and inanity he sees there as art, entertainment, instruction. No longer does he have strength or will to differentiate or to separate himself, and toward bedtime he pats the heads of his children, wishing them long, prosperous, happy lives, just like his own. So be it. It was foreordained by economics, by the threat of enemies and by the hunger and misery of the rest of the world. Let him give himself unto others! Let him put himself into a can of hash, into drum barrels of oil, into woolen underwear, into soy beans, into cash, credit, loans. Let him spread himself over every part of the earth and never once think of the art of poetry which requires merely a mud hut and tablets of clay. Let him set coins in place of his eyes and a baked bean for a nose and a baked potato for a chin, his mouth will be formed of a string bean. Then the world will approach him with delight and he will be both welcomed and devoured.

The poet is dead, long live the poetry! It will arise from the swamps of its own in the form of alligators, in the cries of victims. Poetry will emerge from the ground itself in the stalks of grain and poison ivy. It will be built into the highways and buildings, good hard asphalt and macadam, steel, stone, brick, and a thirty-two hour work week. Poetry will be in the workingman who will take himself home, still in possession of his strength and leisure to murder his wife for an imagined wrong. It could even be a real wrong, but the poetry is in the murder and in the reading about it. And the greatest poem of all will be in the biggest bomb.

1955

Just as I Remember It

Just as I remember it, the still bird black in the snow. I was afraid it was dead. I was sorry. I picked it up and straightened out its legs. It did not respond. Feeling it was dead, nevertheless I placed it in my pocket, thinking the warmth there might help, and I went on ahead on my round of customers to receive their orders for delivery. I had in my arms brown paper bags of meat and chicken for different customers of my father's shop. This was my daily routine after school, and sometimes before school, and often during the nighttime, when I should have been in bed. I would walk the silent streets for about half an hour before I could arrive at my first call. My walk would take me past a cemetery. I'd whistle, I'd sing under my breath and tremble. The night and the silence would lead me to think of intangible, unknown things. I would reach out in my thoughts for the mysterious, because it was the mysterious through which I walked, and to touch it, to know it, and become familiar with it, I felt, would be the next best thing to being safe. And yet the thought of reaching out for it in my mind and perhaps even meeting it as I walked frightened me. I imagined that this itself could be the mysterious, the something that was always behind me and yet threatened me. I may have been scaring myself, but I did not begin with that on my trips past the cemetery alone at night.

The customers would be kind to me, as they opened their doors to me standing on the stoop in front of them. Usually at night I received their orders for the next morning delivery. I have forgotten now how I managed to convey them to my father who would be waiting and resting at home. Nevertheless, I seemed to be doing my work well, for I heard no complaints from him. He would often smile on seeing me return. The customers occasionally would give me a dime for myself, or promise me a dollar present for Christmas. That was one dollar I never did receive, and that, I suppose, could be another reason why all this sticks in my mind. Soon after, my father gave up his shop as a bad business venture. We moved away and I was free to go to school and to come home and read or do as I pleased all the rest of the day. My father had gotten himself a job in his old trade of bookbinding.

The tiny bird, a sparrow perhaps—the memory of it is so far back I can hardly remember the kind of bird, and I suppose it was a sparrow. We had so many of them in the street. The sparrow did not come to life by the time I had returned to the butcher store; and, regretfully, I dug a grave for it and buried it solemnly in the ground. I tried hard to think of this burial as important, I tried to attach to it some meaning, for the occasion was a solemn one for me, without my knowing why or how it was so. There had been life in the bird and then there was none. I associated myself with it, in the cold weather, but could not grasp its meaning. I had been cold walking the streets, and I had been gloomy, away from my friends. In this dead, soft thing I had the opportunity to express my own self-pity, and yet it was a form of play for me, too. I had grasped at the chance of accomplishing something wonderful—bringing back to life a dead bird. What more than this could one do by playing? When I came back from my round of customers, I reached into my pocket, still hoping, to find this bird dead, my illusion of success too was gone, and solemnly, as if to commemorate the departure of my hopes about play, I buried this dead bird. I did it, though, still at play, still believing in play, in the solemn notion of it now, to commemorate what could not be otherwise than this limitation to our life.

1960s

Merely an Incident

How is it that something like this will never get to be known or reflected on by even one person other than myself, yet will have this power to shape a life, my life, but still a life, a part of the whole, therefore of significance of the whole itself? Only I will think of the injustice that was done, unless I write it down, and then what? What difference will it make to the world pushing ahead like an elephant or, for that matter, what difference to me, raising this elephant? I am being taken and the elephant is on its way somewhere in a rage.

What happened took place before I could have any influence on it at all, happening that quickly, while I watched—rather, standing and in the act of watching generally, so to speak: looking on, as is said, but by that simple, unpremeditated, natural act I was involved and held to blame, at least to have to share the blame in what I had no part at all. Even at this moment, what transpired is vague to me, after these many years of thinking and reliving it, and yet I know definitely I was held to blame along with two others, the actual participants in what happened. A stone was thrown, a window was broken, and I was standing nearby idly. Two who were my friends were having a mild argument between them, a kind of friendly scuffle of words such as two kids will have from time to time to liven up things when the day begins to drag. One throws a stone playfully, intending to miss, and does miss but finds the stone sailing into the window of a restaurant beyond. There is a crash and the two friends run. I who have been looking on with interest while dreaming of my own quiet and separateness from this childish quarrel, I am found standing on the corner facing the smashed window, standing and looking at it. My two friends have disappeared. Their quarrel did not put them to sleep in the manner that I slept while watching them. Rather it had kept them lively and keen, and they ran very quickly, able to sense at once what had happened. My face was familiar to the owner of the restaurant. My father was the neighborhood butcher, and he was informed. Angry at me, my father had to pay for the window while I remained silent. I was not going to betray two friends in order to appease my father of a small matter. I was not going to lose my companionship among boys of my age and interest. My father would be with me always, but my friends would scorn me and I would be left alone. To hold them as friends I had to pay a price, and so in silence I let my father scold me and accuse me of wrongdoing. I let him tell my mother, who because of my silence had to believe him.

What of my friends? I had lost them long ago, soon after this incident moving with my family out of the neighborhood, my father having given up his butcher shop as a poor business to return instead to his original trade of bookbinding. We had to move out of the neighborhood to less expensive rooms. I had lost my friends and I had lost something of my father's opinion of me. Never will I be able to convince him that I did not throw that stone. I have no proof now and likely it is that he has forgotten about the incident. He is an old man near to dying and would not be interested in hearing me recall a matter that could only sound trivial to him now. He certainly would think I am being silly to recall it and perhaps revealing a basic foolishness anyhow, something which could be linked up to stone throwing. No. I have decided not to speak to him about it, to get the stain of guilt from my life. It will be there forever with his death, and so it must be, but it is this that puzzles and saddens me. This incident that has spoiled my life, it seems. I once believed in the validity of the person, the sanctity and the inviolability of the person, and it was this that I was dreaming as I stood apart and watched my friends.

1960s

An Imaginary Dialogue
with Allen Ginsberg

—Now, Allen, my position is a very difficult one. I fully understand and appreciate yours and subscribe to it 100 percent. Something in the way we as a country live is dooming us to extinction in pretty short time, despite prosperity, struggle for Negro rights, efforts to improve living conditions, raise standards, increase comfort, and so on. At the heart of it, I feel, as if I felt it in myself, a weakness, a joylessness with life, and inability or incapacity to make ourselves over into the free and easygoing people we want to be, that we think is our goal as a nation. Why is that? At the very center of it all, our forward activity is a doubt, a stumbling, a weakness of spirit, something that won't speak to us, that shies away and hides itself and weeps, it seems. We hear ourselves as if weeping within, and we listen and shout encouragement. See, we now have medicare; soon we'll have lifetime pension beginning at age twenty-five, right after getting your Ph.D. No work, no worry, just spend your time thinking and loving and perhaps doing something very great that will live forever. Yeah, yeah, that's what we tell to that weeping inside, but it just falls silent and refuses to answer even by sign language. We are left as in an empty hall, shouting to make echoes.

—I'm happy.

—Yes, you are. You receive clothes, food, lodging from friends and people who don't know you, nor even know what your work stands for. They help you just because it seems to help them. They feel free at that moment of some incubus pressing upon them, and as they give to you they smile in relief themselves and cheer you on. Is it guilt? I don't know. I'd say rather it was that thing in us that refuses to stop crying or falls silent when we talk to it. As we forget ourselves, it seems to sneak out; it seems to take control of us and make us do things that in our ordinary routine life could never happen. It could never be thought of. We'd keep adding up that column of figures by which we earn our keep.

—I'm really sorry for you.

—Then I do have your sympathy. I have been describing myself to you, Allen. It's that difficult for me to live, but you may want to know why I must keep living this way. I don't have an answer. I just know that if I were to stop the ordinary things I do I wouldn't know how to go on to the extraordinary things, that which really I crave. I would stand absolutely still, dumbfounded, shocked by myself, frightened, and ready to die. I'd feel I had left earth and was absolutely without foothold. I think I'd feel myself hurtling into space, forever lost to men and to myself. This is what I imagine when I start to project myself in rebellion against my ordinary existence. I do not think I am suited at all to do extraordinary things, and that, to me, is what is so extraordinary in itself, that I should think and know and appreciate and subscribe 100 percent to your way of living, but find myself totally paralyzed when it comes to following in your footsteps.

—You can feed me, if you wish.

—To the best of my ability. I will give you everything I can spare. I will leave nothing extra for myself. I have promised myself that and I have been doing exactly that. When I talk about you, I say nothing but praise. I compare you with the saints. I call you a modern saint, a man who could lead us to salvation, who could quiet the weeping within us and make that lonely voice laugh and even speak to us to tell us how to live, but how, Allen, how; this I don't know, though I keep feeling it can surely happen.

—Come and make love to me.

—It would not be true of me, but perhaps you are saying that I must give my love to men. Perhaps you are right, though I have no way of knowing. I have often thought about it and have found the thought repellent, if curious, and yet there are men who are unable to resist the thought and discover a life there for themselves; but, to speak further, can it be said that the love between two men can accomplish that which the love between man and woman fails to do? Is there not something further you would say that binds you to a saintly attitude toward life? Is it not possible that you have learned something of the nature of love as men and women learn from each other that has led you to an even higher plane? Few, very few men and women escape the abrasions of love. In their middle lives they are worn out from its hard, rough path and look forward to the rest of their lives with loathing, as they look on all the rest of the world with loathing and sing a bitter, lonely song inside, this voice that weeps inside and falls silent when addressed.

—You ask so many questions and then answer each one yourself, as if I should stand around and be your audience; but I forgive you, as I forgive myself my own problems. My saintliness is my burden, as to be bitter and despairing is yours. I have my doubts and rise to crush in me my goodness and charity toward others, my tolerance and love even for the bombers of peasants and the skilled torturers seeking information. So do you, as now you rise to condemn in yourself your lonely voice of disillusion and defeat in a search for relief and beauty. Such is your blessing, as I have mine. We are not opposite ends of experience but meet in rebellion and doubt. As you would seek for the truth, the whole truth of existence, doubting its center in despair, I rise to question my saintliness and would add to it a cautiousness, a wish to discern evil from good and act accordingly, but I am defeated. When I begin to make distinctions, my heart fails me, my goodness falters. I am without resources any longer for love and charity, and I begin to cringe. My way is fixed. If I see evil being done, I invite it to be done unto myself, thus to show how little it matters in the workings of the world which is formed of blessedness, our ultimate love above all. I am a lover of man for the same reason. There is no evil that cannot be resolved in me and so I sincerely love man, if this be the evil worst of all, or as I hurl myself before cops and militarists in protest at my government's ways to kill and maim. A revolutionary am I? A subversive character, an insidious moment in our proud history of freedom? A pervert, a decadent, a man without scruples or conscience, given over to riots and orgies, who would pull down the fabric of decency to establish anarchy and death? All this may be so, but only when seen in isolation from the world. I would prove to you that all this sordidness, as you might say, exists for us all and in us all in such forms you cannot recognize or refuse to acknowledge, and that such actions as you take to suppress peoples, crush liberties, enslave whole nations are in themselves the anarchy and death which in me you detest and decry. I show you what there is in you and by which you live your right-teous self-despair, false because you cannot acknowl-edge from where it comes. I am a saint, as you say I am, because I have acknowledged everything and practice everything to discover there is no ultimate evil, because all of it is man and man cannot be called evil while he lives, but there is death and that is his final perspective from which he must act to affirm himself even more strongly in his nature to be always known to himself, so that death is not his only destination or fate, but he may live to praise and be praised in himself as of the totality of existence.

—I agree.

—Then come and embrace me as two men who have known the worst of it and can live to speak to each other in oneness forever. This is the only meaning of my embrace.

—So be it, for life is one for us both.

(And they embrace and go their separate ways.)

1960s

V

One Man's View

To speak of modern literature, I must only speak for myself as poet, of my experiences, but in speaking about myself I expect to be able to give some insight into the nature and direction of modern literature, since poetry is and has been in the past the ground of growth for modern literature. Why this is so is interesting in itself and a clue to the nature of modern literature. Poetry, like no other written art, deals nakedly with the sensibilities. It has no other means since poetry is the art of emotions. We can say the same of fiction to an extent but within the context of narration and character. Poetry meets the emotions head on, especially as written today. Without the emotions plainly staring us in the face, or assaulting or chanting to our ears we do not have contemporary poetry. There is metaphysical poetry which could claim to be a poetry of the intellect, but then we are speaking of a poetry that existed and was being written in the seventeenth century. We can speak of Wallace Stevens as a metaphysical poet whose emotions are shielded by a vast army of philosophical lyricism on the nature of man and of existence, but Stevens is the exception that proves the case.

Look around at poetry being written today and what does one see but the expressive, highly charged feelings of an Allen Ginsberg, or the muted sorrows of a Robert Lowell, or the anger and self-destructiveness of an Anne Sexton or Sylvia Plath. We can think of Adrienne Rich as an intellectual poet, but a close look at her work reveals exactly the opposite. She is a passionate exponent of a highly emotional issue, women's rights. Further, there is Robert Bly and James Wright who make feeling—for Bly it is the unconscious—their prime source of poetry. And so with this brief survey, which could be extended for pages, we can say that poetry today is carrying out in magnificent style its own natural tendency, as it has done for centuries past, evoking the exact feelings universal in the society of its day, and if metaphysical poetry is still being written in this country it can only have as its roots the sensibility of the poet in the society in which he or she lives and writes, with the powerful undercurrent of feeling guiding the metaphysical structure. That is an axiom of our day.

Now it is this particular truth that leads to the next step in my discussion which is this: How then does poetry reveal the nature of modern literature? At this point I will make what will seem a divergence from my theme. I must speak of my own experience as a poet since the beginning of my career. I began with a deep sense of morality and mystery at the same time. The morality was directed toward society, about which I had drawn the conclusion at a very early age, even before I had begun to write, that at the very least it was imperfect. Men stole from men, men abused and killed other men and women, and children too were not immune to cruelty toward one another. As a child, I would often be driven to tears by my disappointment in my playmates, especially as I experienced one of their cruel or thoughtless acts; and I would have to stand by and watch and suffer the tears of my playmates who were taking their turn at feeling the thoughtless or conscious cruelty of their friends. Of course, there were times when we could laugh or joke among ourselves, but with an edge to it. Already we were being conditioned through our own acts toward one another for what was to become the life of our adult years. It was to be hard and relentless in its demands on us to stay strong and balanced in the midst of a chaos of undirected blows and pleasures. This was the mystery that each of us took home to brood on in solitude in our beds and with which we fell asleep. For me, and perhaps for my friends too, this mystery involved the idea of a God who supposedly presided over our destinies and our welfare. If he existed then he surely was part of the mindless acts we as children perpetrated and had to endure from others. It was a mystery to me that such a God who was being worshipped in synagogues and churches throughout the world could exist, as if He were the benefactor who had given us our lives out of His goodness, rather than being the source, if He did exist, of our confusion toward Him and toward ourselves. After all, we had been told over and over again in these houses of worship that God was the fount of all our joys and pleasures and in Himself was perfect. Why, then, I would ask myself in my childish way, was not this perfection that was God translated into perfect children out of His goodness? Why were we given that nature which only served to weaken and confuse us toward Him and toward ourselves? It was a real and profound mystery for me in those early years and it translated itself later, as I began to write, into many poems of supplication for His mercy and for His kindness of being in the natures of all my friends, and especially in myself, noting how mindless and self-centered I could be.

The poems were attempts at clarification of my dilemma, and sometimes I would affirm Him and His works in terms of absolute faith and hope, and at other times in terms of absolute despair. Each mood would depend on the situation I would find myself in, and so I could see that I was being torn apart between two opposing and irreconcilable positions, neither of which could wholly satisfy me emotionally and intellectually. In either position I could find a qualification or a modification that would completely undermine that position from which I would try to understand and accept the world and myself in it. For example, I could convince myself that in each bitter experience there was a lesson to be learned with which to guard myself during the next similar occurrence, and in each ecstatic moment of revelation I could fall back upon the cautionary thought of what tomorrow might bring. I was confusing both positions, rendering them meaningless and, as a result, useless to me.

I was to discover in yet later years, as I was beginning to read more widely than in school, that my intellectual and emotional stalemate was a classical crisis, as was my acute dilemma toward discovering a sense of order in the world and in myself. I was reading such authors as Nietzsche, Schopenhauer, Kierkegaard, all of whom gave me to realize that I was deep in the religious tradition of doubt and self-examination, but whatever comfort I could draw from their mental and emotional stress, it was not enough to resolve my unhappiness. Mine persisted because it was unique to me and peculiarly my own. I was here and now, and they were in the past, free of their burdens. I had all the anguish yet to go through and the world was still acting as they had experienced it, without their solving its difficulties for themselves either. This adult world was my childhood world raised to an even greater intensity, and its confusion and chaos systematized, as it seemed to me, on an even wider scale by mature men and women. And so the poetry I was then writing began to reveal an implicit recognition of the absence of God, and I had begun to concentrate, instead, on the nature of man himself, without God. I had developed into what was called then in literary jargon a poet of realism.

I would try to resolve the loss of God, in whose contradictions and lapses I could no longer have faith, by a belief in the innate need of man for his fellow man, if only out of an innate desire to survive, a survival that was, I believed, motivated by a need for the love of his fellow man, without which he could not survive. This was to be an optimistic realism, inspired in part by the writings of Whitman, whom I had just begun to read as an antidote to Schopenhauer and company; but I soon came to realize that my attraction to Whitman's poetry, especially at that time, came precisely from his own attraction to the idea of the perfectly comradely God, the One who was invisible. In other words, he too was grounded on the belief in an assumed good out of the hand of a beneficent force, no longer the personal God of our fathers. In brief, it was traditional religion translated by me into the abstract, humanist, scientific terminology of our day, a pathetic disguise for my loss. So I was still clinging to a received faith, but in the form of some undefinable and as yet mysterious source.

Let me pause here for a moment to suggest how in this foreshortened version of my intellectual and emotional growth I had begun to recognize the features of modern literature, and how they were asserting themselves in me as poet. Already I had read Karl Marx, as well as Whitman, two giants who could not have been more different from each other in spirit and form but together were reinforcing my new, growing optimistic view, though to my unhappiness in the midst of this development I already was feeling in my deepest self that this optimism that had taken over in my poetry was not to be the last answer to my intellectual and emotional dilemma. Since I really was not satisfied with my received religion in its scientific, humanist dress, would I have to abandon a sense of order entirely? It was the question gnawing at me from beneath everything else. What could exist for me with which to make life bearable and worth living in its confusion? I was fearful of the answer that already I could sense in the life around me that yet persisted in its headlong, mindless way in the manner that I lived through as a child. There had been no reasoning to it then, and never an argument or plea that could persuade it from its impulsive, terrifying path. The present was my childhood lived all over again but even worse now because it was without hope of relief. I was living it because there was nothing else, and so I was not shielded from this life either. I was horrified in my deepest self. The optimism of my poems began to lose its glow for me, and I was helpless to stem the tide of raw, naked feeling that was beginning to assert itself in them. I was the naked man with the club in hand facing the enemy, and I had only the truthfulness to life in my poems with which to defend myself from being overwhelmed; so I would be the man for all seasons, prepared for anything, believing in nothing and glorifying only in action, action alone, as it was lived by all.

It became a principle of my poems, nearly to the exclusion of thought or feeling itself, and this, as I read further into the moderns after Whitman, paralleled a development in contemporary poetry, called objectivist poetry, emphasizing image and vivid situations over thought or emotion. For me, it was a way to go because I could see no point in pursuing an idea or feeling in poetry for its own sake, when in reality neither feeling nor thought had a life beyond the moment of its birth. Action spoke louder than words, paralleling contemporary life, and in objectivist poetry it was a way of dealing honestly, and therefore safely, with this life.

Now, strangely enough, I am no longer interested in action in poetry. Now, from long personal experience, action in itself has become a disguised form of despair for me, as it had always been without my acknowledging it. In the life of drift that most of us live, action is some sort of absolute value that has taken the place of our lost traditional values. Action as we perform it today, even in its most heroic form, is nearly sterile. One has only to look around to see how fruitless and even dangerous to life it can become. Now there is only feeling for me, and there is no metaphysic in it at all, unless you would say that the values I place on feeling, truth to feeling, feelings truthfully presented, are in themselves a kind of metaphysic, a way of receiving, understanding, and accepting. Yes, that may be so; but the emphasis is on feeling, on one's relationship to oneself and to others. But this does not exclude the world around me. On the contrary, it absorbs this world and brings it into focus as the world on which we must dwell to act authentically with our feeling selves. It does not exclude the cruelties, the mindlessness, the phony pleasures, the relentless search among ourselves and from ourselves for aggrandizement of one sort or another, for gain and domain, all that which lies beneath the surface and is the motor force of our undirected, uninformed, and impulsive lives. All this, and even worse, is within the sphere of feeling, and I write of it as much as I can survey in myself and in others. I made no absolute judgments, except where I believe there is pretense to other than being oneself at a given moment. I write for exactness of feeling; and I know that ultimately feeling must and does encompass and body forth those ideas and values that we bring to life anyway, through the response we have toward life in its specific instances, and the response is through feeling.

In other words, we project ideas in their emotional forms. In poetry this translates itself into the work of the unconscious, or as close as the conscious can come to touching upon and projecting the unconscious. Here I am describing the main principle of modern literature. There are exceptions as always, but as I stated earlier, they prove the case. Modern literature no longer portrays man in his conflict with God or in partnership with God, or God in conflict with man. We are through with that kind of metaphysical confrontation. It is man in his relationship to man that makes for modern literature as man looks out upon the cosmos to discover no God exists but space and time and other forms of life than ours and the predictable end of the cosmos itself. In modern literature, we do not despair, as we did when we were faced with the invisible, unpredictable God. We exult that we have found our source of being, our source of life and happiness, pleasure and tragedy in the cosmos itself, which too is finite like ourselves; and we exult that we live to write and speak of it in the freedom that is part of the freedom of the cosmos itself, for we live in freedom from a crippling illusion. It is the new religion, if you will, ours to do with as we please and as we change. This is the spirit of modern literature.

You have been patiently following my recital of a long, developing career, but as I stated at the start of this discussion, it was with the intention of giving an insight into the nature and direction of modern literature, as seen through the eyes and experience of a contemporary poet, and I think it is especially appropriate to have done so when viewed historically. In 1932, at the age of eighteen, I stepped out of high school into the worst economic, social, and political disaster of our times, the Great Depression. It was enough to turn upside down, inside out, and junk everything that we had cherished and practiced in complete faith that these practices and beliefs would last forever. They did not, not for me, and not for the millions who were caught as I was in that catastrophe. That there is a one-to-one relationship, a direct current between the Great Depression and modern writing is too great a claim, but that the Depression did set the climate for profound, lasting change in literature is undoubted and, as I have tried to show, did have its affect on me.

Among the poets who came of spiritual and poetic age during those years and later grew into acknowledged modern masters, I could name a dozen at least, each from whom I have learned and taken strength and courage to see me through crises. Many of these important poets came before me to lay the basis for my poetry, and let me name two who stand out at this moment in my mind for my closeness to them in spirit and method: Charles Reznikoff and William Carlos Williams, both once dear friends of mine, and now gone, but with me still for what they yet have to say to me that is so typically and refreshingly modern, and with which I am wholly identified. I will first read from a poem by Charles Reznikoff. It is titled "Separate Way," taken from his selected volume, *By the Waters of Manhattan.*

> Take no stock in the friendly words of friends,
> for in such kindness all their kindness ends;
> we go our separate ways to death.
>
> The love of father or of mother knows
> the fear of sickness, the need of food and clothes,
> but otherwise we go our separate ways to death.

Kiss after kiss of the head beside you on the cushion
but faithful only in its fashion—
we go our separate ways to death.

If you would see the phoenix burn
and in the traffic hunt a unicorn,
well, ride the subway till your death
and hold your job till you are out of breath.
We heard your jokes, your stories, and your songs,
know of your rights and all your wrongs,
but we are busy with our own affairs.

Sorry? O Yes! But after all who cares?
You think that you have something still to say?
Perhaps. But you are growing old, are growing gray.
And we are too.
We'll spare another friendly word for you;
and go our separate ways to death.

Here is a poem that already in 1935 could anticipate
the gathering dissonance with which we characterize
contemporary writing today, alienated from its deepest
beliefs. Reznikoff was to come in his middle age to a re-
valuation of his position toward his religion, but it was
at best a marginal reconciliation, with its emphasis on
his origins as a Jew, without especial concern for the
God of his people. He was too much the man of this
century to allow himself the luxury of an unknowable
and unavailable God, and this poem, as many, many later
poems of his with even greater force, describes a malaise
of the human spirit that can only be identified with these
times.

The next poet from whom I will read is William Carlos
Williams, whose influence has spread to every corner of
the Western world to shape its spirit and give it form. I
will read from the famous long poem, *Paterson*, book
three, part III.

Fire burns; that is the first law.
When a wind fans it the flames

are carried abroad. Talk
fans the flames. They have

maneuvered it so that to write
is a fire and not only of the blood.

The writing is nothing, the being
in a position to write (that's

where they get you) is nine tenths
of the difficulty: seduction

or strong arm stuff. The writing
should be a relief,

relief from the conditions
which as we advance become—a fire,

a destroying fire. For the writing
is also an attack and means must be

found to scotch it—at the root
if possible. So that

to write, nine tenths of the problem
is to live. They see

to it, not by intellection but
by sub-intellection (to want to be

blind as a pretext for
saying, We're so proud of you!

A wonderful gift! How do
you find the time for it in

your busy life? It must be a great
thing to have such a pastime.

But you were always a strange
boy. How's your mother?)

—the cyclonic fury, the fire,
the leaden flood and finally
the cost—
Your father was *such* a nice man,
I remember him well

Or, Geeze, Doc, I guess it's all right
but what the hell does it mean?

There you have it all, brought home to the poet him-
self, the alienation of the spirit from its very self in the
form of the average man, the man of America who can-
not and does not want to realize that he is listening and
bearing witness to his own true nature in the poet who
is standing before him: Divorce, as Williams said so fa-
mously, is the knowledge of our times. The tragedy of
it, the cruelty and indifference to which it gives rise in
the man who lives next door. You have in this poem the
quintessence of the modern, and if there is anything I
would illustrate further in myself, it may all be found in
the work of such poets as Reznikoff and Williams. You
can find it in many, many other writers as well and that
is why we can have this as a subject to discuss. It exists
by virtue of the presence of these witnesses, of which I
proudly count myself one.

Still, we must not end on this tragic note because there
is yet another stream to the contemporary sensibility as
I pointed out just a little while back. We have among us
poets such as Robert Bly. Let me read part of a short
prose poem from his most recent volume, *This Body Is
Made of Camphor and Gopherwood.*

A man and woman sit quietly near each other. In the snow-
storm millions of years come close behind us, nothing is

lost, nothing rejected, our bodies are equal to the snow in energy. The body is ready to sing all night, and be entered by whatever wishes to enter the human body singing. . . .

This is the other side of our spirit. We live to celebrate our minimal existence. It has come to us from the known cosmos and will return to it in time, but we will never be lost or forgotten, the finite cosmos is our being. All that is tragic or sordid in man is transcended in the knowledge that he can be cleansed; he is the snow that falls upon a wintery night. Bly is our foremost visionary poet, and knowing the terrible bitter, bloodiness of the world (He has written our greatest anti-Vietnam war poem, "The Teeth Mother Naked at Last"), knowing this and much worse, encompassing the truths of a Williams and a Reznikoff, he stands forth with his smile of peace and eternal satisfaction in being here. Bly is modern literature standing on its feet and walking into the future.

Think of Whitman speaking to us today. I misjudged him as a youth. I saw him only in a social context in the years of the Depression that were filled with stress. But he was and is much more than a social poet. He is one who felt himself eternal, at least as long as we were around on this earth, and even beyond, as he ventured to say; and because he saw we were one in spirit and destiny he did not despair. He wrote for us to take heart, to live together even as we are apart. This is how he speaks to me today. The feeling that I have from his work, the feeling that his work allows me to have toward my fellow man is one of peace and solidarity. We shall overcome, and that is modern, as modern as the ancient hills, but now it is here with us to take and use well. Such are the poems to be written, and they are being written in the farthest corners of the earth, and right here now.

I have gone on long enough and so allow me to conclude with a prose poem of my own with which, after all, I could have begun and ended these remarks, without anything else said between.

Did you know that hair is flying around in the universe? Hair trimmed from beards in barber shops, from mustaches at the mirror, from underarms, from crotches, legs and chests—human hair. It all gets dumped into a fill-in space and then the wind gets at it and sails it back into the cities and towns and villages, right through your open windows during summer and even during winter down your chimney. Hair, brown, black, red, white, grey, and yellow. They get all mixed up and you find them on your pullover sweater and you wonder who did you come up against with yellow hair which you happen to like and you dream of its actually having happened that you were in touch with a person with yellow hair.

That's not the whole of it. Think of walking through the street on a windy day or even on a calm, balmy day. The hair is floating all around you and you are walking through perhaps an invisible or fine mist of cut hairs. Black, brown, red that you would not have cared to touch in a million years because you associate them with certain kinds of faces and behavior but there are the hairs of these people touching and clinging to you, as if trying to tell you that hair is every-where and everybody has it and that it's hopeless to try to pick black or brown or red off your sleeves but not yellow hair.

It would be an act of insanity. You need to pick them all off or none and let yourself be covered by them all, like a new kind of fur coat or perhaps a new hairy skin to protect you from the weather. Hair of all colors. What a pretty sight that would make, wouldn't it, and you would have a coat of many colors, and I bet you would be proud of it, especially if you saw everyone else wearing a coat of many colors. How about that? Because people cut their hair and let it fly out over the world where they land on everyone and everyone is sharing in the coat of many colors.

1978

296